The Age of Guilt

THE AGE OF GUILT

THE SUPER-EGO IN THE ONLINE WORLD

MARK EDMUNDSON

Yale
UNIVERSITY PRESS

New Haven and London

Yale University Press books may be purchased in quantity for educational,
business, or promotional use. For information, please e-mail sales.press@
yale.edu (U.S. office) or sales@yaleup.co.uk (U.K. office).

Set in Gotham and Adobe Garamond type by IDS Infotech, Ltd.
Printed in the United States of America.

Library of Congress Control Number: 2022942193
ISBN 978-0-300-26581-1 (hardcover : alk. paper)

A catalogue record for this book is available from the British Library.

This paper meets the requirements of ANSI/NISO Z39.48-1992
(Permanence of Paper).

10 9 8 7 6 5 4 3 2 1

For William and Ashley
Hope

Contents

CONTENTS

CONTENTS

Preface: The Unwelcome Guest

Imagine being ruled by a tyrant king.

The king is crude to the point of vulgarity, judgmental in the extreme, and bitterly punitive. He likes to sound reasonable, though he's anything but. He wants you, and if possible everyone else, to do what he says all the time. The king is unable to enjoy himself except through acts of meanness and even cruelty. He has no capacity for humane joy or fun. He's incapable of a good time.

"All deities reside in the human breast," said William Blake. To which we might add that demons do, too.

Blake, one of the three great Romantic poets along with Wordsworth and Whitman, had a few names for the rogue king that resides in the human breast. He called him Urizen and Nobodaddy, or sometimes the Spectre. Blake was an illuminating anatomist of the human soul: he understood dimensions of himself (and perhaps of us all) that we still have not come to terms with.

Who are these creatures—who are Urizen and Nobodaddy and the Spectre? They differ in certain ways, but they are all at war against the ethical and imaginative power of the human spirit. They enforce conformity and fear. Urizen draws confining circles—horizons—that keep human aspiration in check. Nobodaddy is an image of the Hebrew Bible's God at his most punitive, sterile, and cruel—he is Nobody's Daddy, but Blake feels we adopt him as a paternal figure of authority for our own reasons. The Spectre is fearful, fretful, jealous, and competitive: he hates what is most loving and open about the self and throttles it when he can. He is the ultimate figure of self-defeating self-protection. "My Spectre around me night and day," says Blake, "Like a wild beast guards my way." The Spectre oppresses the interior figure that Blake calls the Emanation: a being that embodies the individual's hope for love and imaginative achievement.

The debased god Urizen, the cruel Nobodaddy, the looming Spectre: to Blake the psyche can be a house haunted by fears and anxieties—perhaps above all, by harsh self-judgment. Blake's inquisitorial figures, different as they are, constantly torment the self for deeds that do not merit condemnation, and sometimes even for deeds worth praising. Where do these figures come from? How do they emerge? Blake seems to think they have a social and cultural origin. He is living in a monarchical age that has yet to throw off feudalism. It's also an age of reductive empirical science, not of imagination, in which the reigning cultural figures are conservatives like Alexander Pope and Samuel Johnson. People tend to believe there is nothing terribly new under heaven and that the best literary art consists in "what oft was thought but ne'er so well expressed." To Blake, many consequential truths remain undiscovered. He hopes to find them, if he can overcome the resistance of his interior demons.

Blake is right. A power that judges us, often irrationally, and demeans us, often without cause, does abide within us. Sometimes it operates consciously, letting us feel the dark pressure of self-condemnation. But it can also work outside the circle of conscious understanding.

Sigmund Freud, who almost surely never read Blake, believed he had uncovered such an agency. He called it the super-ego or over-I. (*Über-ich* is the German term.) As a culture, we've lost contact with what Freud and Blake had to say about this inner power, and the loss has been damaging. Cultures do travel backwards. After the fall of Rome, crucial classical texts were lost to the world. Now, as a literate and literary culture is displaced by a visual, electronic one, we are in danger of losing contact with a consequential piece of wisdom about the human psyche. Call it the Spectre, call it the super-ego: a force that judges and condemns lives in us all. There are manifold ways to contend with this force, and I'll be discussing them in these pages. But to deal well with the Spectre or the super-ego, one must first take seriously the possibility that it exists.

The philosopher Ludwig Wittgenstein was transfixed by Freud, calling his work a "very powerful mythology." And we might think of what Freud offers as myth. The ego and the id are no more real than Apollo and Dionysus. But we can learn more about our lives and the life of the world from the mythology of the ancient Greeks than from many works that set out to tell us the literal, binding truth.

The ultimate test of Freud's thinking is its power to illuminate and transform. Does the myth of the super-ego (call it that for now) ring true to our experience? Does it persuasively describe consequential aspects of life that we have yet to fully understand? Does it add, to take a phrase from the critic R. P. Blackmur, to our stock of available reality? If so, we want to know if the myth can lead us forward to a better life: more sane, less afflicted, more useful to others. Does it allow us to understand ourselves and to change life for the better? To borrow a criterion from William James, is it good in the way of belief?

Freud was sometimes willing to see his work as myth: "the drives," he said once, "are our mythology." But he also believed that empirical science would eventually confirm his educated intuitions and imagining. Scientists are now making such attempts. In a brilliant recent paper on the "entropic brain," Robin L. Cahart Harris and his colleagues argue that there is empirical evidence of an unconscious element of the mind that functions much as Freud said it did. I'm intrigued by such developments but am, at least for now, content to stay with

Wittgenstein's perception: that Freud provided a very powerful mythology. The Greeks gave us Apollo and Dionysus; in the profoundly suggestive *Birth of Tragedy,* Friedrich Nietzsche drew on Apollo, Dionysus, and an imaginatively revised version of Socrates. Freud the myth-maker offers us the ego, the id, the super-ego, and more.

In the Freudian myth, the super-ego is a fiercely oppressive agency. Yet people now use the concept much differently, employing *super-ego* as a synonym for *conscience.* "My super-ego is going to be unhappy if I don't get my problem sets done," says the student. "I have a strong super-ego, except on Friday and Saturday night," says the man on his way to a party. Freud, however, located our conscious moral standards and creditable hopes in the ego: the super-ego is something else.

Freud sees the super-ego as increasing its grip over time. In his most frequently read book, *Civilization and Its Discontents,* he describes how it gathers strength. Its powers are enhanced by a society that grows constantly more restrictive and more capable of surveillance and punishment. As society compels us to repress aggression, the over-I takes up that anger and directs it at the self. The super-ego is dynamic. A hundred years ago, Freud saw its powers increasing in individuals and in the culture at large. It is hard to imagine that matters have improved.

As a teacher, I see the ravages of the super-ego almost daily. My students are bright, talented, and kind, but oppressed by standards that have been instilled deep within them. They are often overwhelmed with anxiety. They're frequently depressed. Both of these conditions, I believe, can arise from having an internal agency making demands that are virtually impossible to meet. My students take six courses per term, they are in five clubs, they cultivate numberless "friends" online and off-, and at a certain point, usually near the end of the school term, it can become too much. At a time in life when they should be alive with possibility and excited by all they've learned and all that's left to learn, they're riven with anxiety or weighed down by depression. They often tell me that their lives shuttle between anxiety and deep boredom.

Depression takes hold of young people early now. A thoughtful piece in the *Atlantic* tells us that "rates of adolescent depression declined slightly from the early '90s through the mid-aughts. Shortly thereafter, though, they started climbing, and they haven't stopped. Many studies, drawing on multiple data sources, confirm this; one of the most recent analyses, by Pew, shows that from 2007 to 2017, the percentage of 12-to-17 year olds who had experienced a major depressive episode in the previous year shot from 8 percent to 13 percent—meaning that, in the span of a decade, the number of severely depressed teenagers went from 2 million to 3.2 million." Things get no better when young people arrive at college.

Few of my students have heard of the super-ego. None of them believe that coming to terms with one's inner agency of authority, and maybe transforming it, are crucial to attaining a measure of happiness in the world. They simply suffer on, unarmed with the basic resources that Blake, Freud, and a few others offer.

They are in some measure victims of the wholesale cultural repudiation of Freud. In the current environment, a major thinker with some bad ideas—and Freud had at least a few—is dismissed out of hand. To be worthy of serious hearing, one sometimes feels, an authority figure has to approach moral perfection. This in itself is a form of super-ego thinking. It's self-righteous and ultimately self-defeating. One might say, perhaps a little fancifully, that the super-ego–style repudiation of Freud enhances the super-ego's power by persuading people to ignore it.

We first hear about this agency of the psyche in Freud's 1914 essay "On Narcissism," though he does not actually name it until 1923. Freud says that patients suffering from paranoia tell him they feel they are being watched by an independent agency that criticizes them constantly. This force, which is largely administered through the voice, sometimes issues a running commentary on the individual and what he is thinking and doing—and also on who and what he is. The commentary is not kind. Says Freud, "Patients . . . complain that all their thoughts are known and their actions watched and supervised; they are informed of the functioning of this agency by voices which characteristically speak to them in the third person."

Then Freud makes a leap that puts him in the poetic territory of Blake. The complaint of the paranoiac, he says, "is justified; it describes the truth. A power of this kind, watching, discovering and criticizing all our intentions, does really exist." Then the critical turn: "Indeed, it exists in every one of us in normal life." A force that watches and comments and judges, most of all judges, is a factor in everyone's inner life. It will be almost a decade before Freud begins to call this power the super-ego and affirms it as a third element in the psyche, along with the ego and the id. From then on, until his death in 1939, Freud is preoccupied with the problems of authority and accordingly with the problem of the super-ego.

We are all, he will tell us in the 1923 volume *The Ego and the Id*, in a difficult fix: the ego or conscious mind must navigate a perilous external world and deal with the pressure of desire from the id, the seat of the instincts. But it must also contend with the force of judgment and prohibition that originates in the super-ego. Often, especially among the more socialized, this force becomes unendurably harsh: it punishes us for transgressions, but its sense of transgression is crude. It assumes we are children in need of a harsh parent. Not only does the super-ego punish us for actual trespasses, it punishes us for sins we only imagine committing.

The super-ego is not moral, it is supra-moral. The ego, the thinking self, may approve a certain action: perhaps indulgence in some sexual pleasure. But the over-I does not concur. The self, the ego, may give its approval to a homosexual connection, let us say, but the super-ego may still become enraged. There follows punishment. The punishment can be conscious and perceptible: a voice that both is and is not the subject upbraids him as a degenerate and even an evil-doer. But the ego, which has no problem with homosexuality, condones and encourages the act. This does not matter—the super-ego will have its say and take its revenge. Sometimes, Freud says, the super-ego exerts itself unconsciously. Its punitive rants are unheard. But people suffer anxiety, depression, or psychosomatic illness.

People are implanted young with super-egos, be they weak, strong, or in between. The cultural context sometimes strengthens and sometimes weakens the punitive super-ego. How could it be otherwise? Culture is inconsistent. At times a loose and tolerant ethos reigns, as in the America of the late 1960s and, perhaps more so, the 1970s. At other times, for reasons that are not easy to determine, a more stringent morality takes hold. At present, among people who think of themselves as educated and liberal, a potent streak of morality or even self-righteous moralism has emerged. They are always on the alert for infractions against right-thinking and correct action. The judgments go on and on, often triggered by very little. An era of oppressive morality? Living amidst the ostensibly enlightened, it is easy to imagine so.

Why has the super-ego become ascendant in culture now? One suspects there are many reasons, but surely the Internet is a primary one. What began as a zone of free speculation and open exchange has become a site of ridicule, condemnation, and character destruction. The archetypal action on the Internet now appears to be scapegoating. The mob finds a transgressor—someone who in the past or present broke the codes of current speech or thought—and goes after him. The objective is to do as much damage as possible in as little time as possible.

The prize is to disgrace the victim, and to rob him of his livelihood. This is a victory for the super-ego–inspired mob. How the Internet became the culture's chief manifestation of the over-I is uncertain, but no one can doubt that it is. Almost every instance of super-ego tyranny that I'll examine in this book is yoked in some way to the Internet.

Freud and Blake tell us something similar about an overaggressive moral streak: it can become ravingly unbalanced and it can take over an individual. Nietzsche knew this as well. In *Thus Spake Zarathustra*, he warns us to distrust those who talk obsessively of justice. The hangman peers from their countenances. They long to be judges. They would love to be Pharisees too, if they had the power. Nietzsche is being hyperbolic, but he understands that beyond a certain point, judgment becomes a form of sickness. "Distrust all in whom the impulse to punish is powerful."

Surely there are individuals in the world who have authentically high moral standards and are devoted to reform. All honor to them. They tend to be modest, humane, gentle people, intolerant of oppressive laws and customs, but tolerant of the foibles of other human beings and aware of their own.

Too many of our contemporaries bear the signs of possession by the super-ego. They are, like the super-ego itself, immune to irony, void of humor, unforgiving, prone to demand harsh punishments. They align themselves with super-ego–affiliated institutions. They see deans, CEOs, and human resource departments as vehicles for visiting punishment on transgressors. All too many situations devolve to black and white, with no hint of an intervening shade. There is no forgiveness and no redemption.

There's a well-known story about Martin Luther King. When he was on the street leading a demonstration, he passed a screaming White woman, who spat at him. He walked up to her, looked her in the eye, and said simply, "You're much too beautiful to do something like that." The super-ego is baffled by such a story. Why would any-one want to brush off an offense and try to lead someone to higher ground? Where is the enjoyment in that? The pleasure of condemna-tion is not to be surrendered lightly. Those unfortunates who are pos-sessed by the super-ego live in a world of punishment and discipline, with too little room for grace—for themselves or others.

Blake, Freud, Nietzsche: perhaps they know us better than we know ourselves. All three set up the problem of judgment and con-demnation as critical for human beings. They recognized that in the normal course of life, people need to make judgments. They need to evaluate experience. Perhaps at times they need to condemn this or that. But all three understand that people often get drunk on judg-ment: drunk on criticism, of themselves and of others. This is a ten-dency we must understand and in time struggle with.

In a marvelous essay on self-criticism, Adam Phillips, a follower of Freud, writes about what it would be like if the super-ego left the confines of the psyche and went out into the world as an individual. It's a scenario that would have pleased Blake, who liked to imagine aspects of the spirit embodied as characters. In Phillips's rendering, the over-I turns up at a party. He goes around criticizing everyone. He speaks in a dead monotone. He's a complete bore, no one likes him, and he has to go home. (I elaborate on Phillips rather freely here.) He is, as Phillips says, "strikingly unimaginative; both about morality and about ourselves—the selves he insists on diminishing."

But I fear that when the over-I goes to a party today he finds more super-egos. They ask him who he thinks the administration's biggest racist is. They exchange antisexist jokes. He tells them about his new Twitter campaign to rid the world of speech crimes and thought crimes to boot. He's the life of the party. Or maybe it's better to say that he's the death of it, which really charms everybody. It's that kind of party.

It's easy to smile at such figures. But not only do they inflict pain, they are in pain themselves. It would be helpful to all if they were delivered from it.

Phillips is one of the few public intellectuals who takes the super-ego seriously. Another is the Slovenian philosopher Slavoj Žižek. Žižek follows Jacques Lacan, who also had a long-standing interest in the idea of the over-I, but he modifies Freud's conception of it. To Žižek, the super-ego is a figure of "obscene enjoyment." It pretends to be virtuous, righteous, an upholder of admirable laws both public and private. It masquerades as a disinterested, even a noble force. But it revels in seeing others punished. Behind a sober, high-minded mien, it takes unmitigated joy in the sufferings of the fallen. And it takes masochistic joy in its own self-lacerations. I must do better, better, better! Says Žižek, "No wonder, then, that Lacan posits an equation between *jouissance* and super-ego: to enjoy is not a matter of following one's spontaneous tendencies; it is rather something we do as a kind of weird and twisted ethical duty."

What's to be done about this unwelcome guest, this Spectre? I think Freud's initial answer would be rather simple: start by experimenting with the idea that it exists. Try out the hypothesis that within you dwells a figure and force that both is and is not yourself. The figure lives to criticize and even condemn you. And—important addition—you sometimes get relief from condemnation by aiming its judgment outside of you. It's a relief to fuse with him and move his attention away from yourself and into the world. But a problem arises. The more you let him play freely, the stronger he gets, so when he once again aims his venom at you, he does so with redoubled force. The solution is to turn him outward again. Drunks tell you that the only real remedy for a hangover is a morning shot of booze: hair of the dog that bit you. As a long-range strategy, this seldom ends well.

The projection of the super-ego outwards also has daunting political effects. It sometimes seems that the judgment the right-thinking sector of the culture visits on the less refined tends to enflame them. They are tired of being judged by their supposed betters, and they respond not by reforming but by becoming more entrenched in their ways. "Evil be thou my Good," they effectively say, and commit themselves to a theatrical backwardness to shock the super-ego–inflamed. They become more Morlock-like to affront the refined, vulnerable, ever-judging Eloi. They too are victims of the super-ego, letting its force in the culture deform their inner and outer lives. As one side grows tighter, more judgmental, more self-righteous, the other grows callous, mean, aggressive in its ignorance.

When you submit to the reign of the super-ego you make the world a more shabbily puritanical place, and you let yourself in for a lot of pain. What is to be done, after you have been willing to admit that Blake and Freud and Nietzsche *could be* right? You might start by asking yourself questions from time to time. As in, What's going on here? Why am I ranting about this or that? Why do I need a daily political tantrum? Why am I walking back and forth in the senate chamber of my mind delivering half-deranged speeches about the turpitude around me? How come the thought of someone voting for a candidate other than my own makes me boil over, flood the stove and the kitchen floor too? More generally, Why am I so damned critical of everybody and myself to boot?

Or you might say, it's possible that this Spectre thing, this super-ego thing, is beginning to act up. It does that. It's a little like a tantrum-prone baby with the values of a tin-pot dictator. When it starts screaming for what it wants—Revenge! Retribution!—one might tell it to calm down and get some sleep. God can take care of righteous judgment. Until I can simmer down and make my judgments sane and thoughtful, I'll try to stay quiet. In the meantime, I'll see if I can't substitute some cool understanding for rancorous judgment.

Where id was, there ego shall be. That was one of Freud's therapeutic slogans. He meant that allowing the repressed desires of the id into consciousness could be conducive to enhanced sanity. Freud believed that when we turn mute inner experience into words, we begin to make progress. There's something about expression that liberates. We can calm down and move with circumspection rather than simply rely on reflex. With the wisdom of Freud (and Blake and Nietzsche) at hand, one might even stop in the midst of a self-righteous rant and say to oneself: I know there's a part of me that tends to irrational raving. It's not good for the objects of my rant and it's not good for me, either. And the more I exercise this inner beast of righteousness, the more ferocious he gets, and when he's done working out on people in the world, he turns against me—and that is not so pleasant.

How many loud patrons of righteousness do you know who have serious problems with depression and anxiety? These conditions are not easy to explain, but one strong possibility is that they arise from the super-ego's rage against the self, the ego. When you slow the over-I down and question its motives and its tactics, you may make progress toward relative sanity and spare yourself needless pain. Where super-ego was, Adam Phillips has said, there ego shall be.

It may be possible to educate the super-ego. One can perhaps turn it from a spirit that denies to one that affirms. Freud speaks not only of a super-ego but also of an ego-ideal. Unluckily for us, he never got around to drawing a firm line between them. Usually he used the terms synonymously. But given time, he might have propounded a full theory of the ego-ideal as a benign form of inner authority. I will offer the beginnings of one in the following pages.

Perhaps the best way to satisfy the drive to reach higher states of being is through the embrace of ideals. We can grasp a feeling of purpose when we commit ourselves to courage or wisdom or compassion or artistic creation. We can try to fulfill classical ideals actively and positively, rather than trying to bully others (and ourselves) into transient forms of virtue. The super-ego is a rather passive agency. It sits on its brass throne like a child in a highchair and pronounces its inane judgments. It makes us and those around us miserable. But if we try to embody ideals rather than enforce conduct, we may end up feeling better.

With the pursuit of ideals, life takes on meaning and coherence. We have something to do with our energy that's worth doing. Some self-awareness about the machinations of the super-ego is a good temporary remedy, but finally, the best response may be to find alternatives to inner sadomasochism through the active pursuit of values worth affirming. Where super-ego was, there ego shall be? That's a good start. Where the over-I was, there action in pursuit of the ideal shall be? That may be yet better.

So far, I've only outlined the theory of the super-ego, sketched its perils, and gestured toward some remedies. (There are surely more.) But the problem, left virtually unaddressed for decades, is more complex than I've suggested. This is true in part because the super-ego often operates unconsciously. Thus diagnosis is more difficult, the elaborations of super-ego sickness more varied, and the cures (perhaps we should speak of tactics instead) more complex and intriguing. A great deal of human possibility might unlock if we were to come to a critical and humane comprehension of the super-ego, and then move beyond its reign to more satisfying, fruitful ways of being in the world.

PART ONE

Diagnoses

What Is the Super-Ego?

It's tempting to begin with a hard-core Freudian definition of the super-ego, and we'll get to one in time. But let's glance back at Adam Phillips's story about how a super-ego would act if it went out in public. To Freud, the super-ego is an aspect of the psyche, an agency, somewhat like the ego and the id. But in Phillips's fable, he has broken loose and is out on his own, roaming the world. He's even turned up at a party. What sort of social presence does he have? He's boring and speaks in a monotone; he exudes depression sauced with anger and is very, very judgmental. He dislikes this and dislikes that and doesn't always tell you quite why. He moves from room to room and person to person, enumerating faults and flaws. No one knows who invited him. No one likes him. But no one has quite the wherewithal to send him home.

Why should anyone believe in the existence of this agency? Why should we be convinced that a force that is often remote from the conscious mind exerts any determining role in our lives and in the culture at large?

The problem is that the super-ego rarely makes itself so palpably manifest as in Phillips's fable. It is, as Freud tells us, often unconscious. We do not have immediate access to it, but it makes its presence felt by creating self-dislike, anxiety, and depression. In some, it creates the need for punishment. It scalds us so badly with criticism, persuades us that we have so radically transgressed, that sometimes the only relief we can find is in arranging for ourselves to be punished, so as to dissolve, alas only temporarily, our quotient of guilt. The super-ego can even drive the individual to suicide.

Freud discovered—if that is the right word—the over-I late in his career. Until about 1914, he was satisfied to see the psyche as divided into two parts, one unconscious, the other not. The id—the seat of the drives and appetites—is largely unconscious. The ego, the thinking self, is conscious. It can contemplate the world and even itself. ("I think, therefore I am," goes Descartes' famous stroke of self-defining self-consciousness.) Through dreams, jokes, and slips of the tongue and pen, the ego catches glimpses (sometimes more than glimpses) of the id. The idea to Freud the therapist in his early phase is to make peace with desires by opening oneself, as far as possible, to the content of the id. A well-tempered and well-tended ego can colonize the id— make it calmer and less insistent—by understanding and accepting its contents. Thus the Freudian mantra: Where id was, there ego shall be.

For Freud, self-knowledge leads to self-acceptance, and thus to the calming of psychological turbulence. Most of Freud's early patients were out of touch with their desires, especially the forbidden erotic desires that "civilized sexual morality" had outlawed. When Freud brought them into contact with the desires repressed within their ids, patients, after some initial shock, tended to feel better. They stopped their compulsive hand-washing; they found themselves able to go out in public; their unexplained fits of weeping became less frequent. Where id was, there ego came to be.

Alas, achieving psychological health was not quite so simple. As time passed and he became a more sophisticated clinician, Freud began to see other obstacles to his patients' achieving relative tranquility. It turned out that acquainting them with their repressed desires, however gradually and sensitively it was done, wasn't enough. It brought some relief, but problems often remained. These patients, whom

Freud at the start had a great deal of trouble helping, were afflicted with an excessive, irrational sense of guilt. Even minor sins sent them into fits of bitter self-accusation.

In some cases, these patients almost seemed possessed. They were inhabited by a spirit that seemed to dislike, even hate them. Something within held them in contempt, issued harsh edicts, made draconian judgments, and seemed to wish for nothing so much as the patients' suffering and even, in what Freud called melancholia, their demise.

The more Freud studied this baseless self-castigation, the more complicated it grew. In time, he came to believe there was a third agency in the psyche. There was not just the I and the it. There was also an element that he called the over-I (usually referred to in English as the super-ego) and its special province was morality. The over-I maintained vigilance over the ego and punished it not only for deeds it took to be immoral, but sometimes for simply imagining such deeds. Nothing could be hidden from the over-I; it had a panoptic presence in the psyche and saw everything that mattered.

The over-I's special domain was morality, much as the id's special domain was desire. But—and here Freud found a curious paradox— the ego was also in charge of administering morals, so in effect people walked through their daily rounds with two moral agents functioning at once. One of them, the ego, could be rational and reflective, and make plausible and more or less consistent judgments about what is right and wrong. But the other did no such thing. The over-I's moral code (if you could so dignify it) was regressive, irrational, inconsistent, and punitive. It was the code a tyrannical father might inflict on a dependent child. In fact the over-I thought of the I as a child, who needed constant disciplining and frequent punishment.

Sometimes the over-I spoke through the patient in bursts of rage. I'm no good! I'm a loser! There's nothing I can do! I see now why everyone hates me. Freud heard those expostulations in therapy, and no doubt sometimes outside it. They were signs of the diseased super-ego asserting itself. But he came to see that such overt signals were only part of the story. Beneath them lay a whole zone of psychic tension that was mostly unavailable to the conscious mind. The super-ego was as much unconscious as the id.

Freud offered his first general description of the over-I in the 1914 paper "On Narcissism." As we've seen, he talked about patients who complained that they were being watched all the time. Some agency of self-consciousness might, for instance, comment on their actions from moment to moment: now he's making the toast, now he's getting the coffee ready for his wife, now he's bringing it up to her in bed. Then Freud makes one of the leaps for which he is famous—and also infamous. The patient is accurate, Freud says; he describes the truth. And then the important turn: such a power exists in us all. We are all under observation and judgment by an invisible and usually unconscious aspect of the psyche. At fraught moments, it may turn up its volume a bit so we can hear what it has to say.

But the over-I has other forms of communication. Anxiety, depression, impotence, stomach troubles, back troubles, and headaches can all be manifestations of the super-ego's profound unhappiness with the individual. For the ego is inadequate. Or rather, it is inadequate from the vantage of the over-I. We are never good enough, never successful enough, never moral enough. And as Freud says, when the over-I is aggrieved, it punishes the ego very harshly.

It does so, he says, by inflicting its hatred. But perhaps more to the point, it punishes the ego by withholding love. As Freud says at one point, to the ego, "living means the same thing as being loved." He even goes so far as to say that the ego, the self, is made out of love, out of being loved. And when one of the main sources of love, the judging faculty that is the super-ego, withholds respect, care, and nurture, the ego becomes anxious and depressed: it loses confidence. The ego can get some love from the outside world; it can make itself attractive to the id (or so Freud says), but a major source of potential approval—a source of life—is the over-I. The hatred of the over-I for the ego is, according to Freud, one of the major causes of psychological suffering.

What is to be done about that suffering?

Psychological health no longer simply entails making peace between ego and id, prudence and desire. Now a third element enters the game. This element, the super-ego, can be ill and often is: that means it raves unreasonably using reason's anointed terms. As the over-I gains power over the I, it becomes angrier and more demanding. The individual becomes weighed down by guilt, anxiety and self-hatred. When that happens, he becomes for all purposes nonfunctional or can function only at half-powers, keeping precarious balance, fighting to rise from bed in the morning, fighting to make it through the day.

In a famous passage from *The Ego and the Id,* Freud observes that the ego is "a poor creature owing service to three masters and consequently menaced by three dangers: from the external world, from the libido of the id, and from the severity of the super-ego. Three kinds of anxiety correspond to these three dangers, since anxiety is the expression of a retreat from danger." In the individual beset by the over-I, the ego loses the ability to arbitrate the world successfully.

Is it possible for a culture to generate a super-ego? Cultures have manners; they have mores; they have ethical systems. Without those, they would not be cultures. Couldn't a culture's ethical system become ill in much the same way that the individual super-ego does? Might it be possible for a culture to become, at least in one major aspect of itself, pathologically judgmental, condemnatory, punitive? Perhaps it can grow ill in the same way that a super-ego–ridden individual can.

A culture can create a false image of authority and worship it. It can set unendurably high standards and enforce them brutally. Culture can be overrun with violent, destructive, sexually reckless impulses, but it can also become a site of puritanical oppression. As we'll see, those two tendencies can even be mutually reinforcing. The violent Morlocks and the prim Eloi can egg each other on.

Says Freud, enticingly and somewhat enigmatically, one's super-ego is not based on one's father but on one's father's super-ego. So an ostensibly mild father can inject a brutally demanding super-ego into a child. He may be outwardly kindly, generous, and permissive. But the child senses that within him is a force at variance with his lenient exterior, and that force is what the child responds to and fears. Many people who are driven hard internally do all they can to hide it. That is sometimes the condition of the benevolent, "enlightened" father.

Our super-egos do not emanate from the parent's immediate persona, nor do they take account of the overall structure of our psyches. As Freud points out, one of the more distressing dilemmas in life is possessing a super-ego that makes demands that one cannot fulfill. The super-ego does not care that you are not smart enough to be a resounding success. It doesn't care that you lack the beauty and charm that could propel you to social ascendancy. It's no matter to the super-ego that you do not have the entrepreneurial imagination to come up with one splendidly lucrative idea after another. The super-ego wants what it wants. It makes demands and if those demands are not met, it exacts punishment. It does this, Freud tells us, even if those demands are impossible to meet. One of the worst possible fates is to live with a large gap between the strength of one's super-ego and one's resources for achievement.

The result of unmet super-ego demands is sickness. The super-ego punishes the ego and turns it into an anxious, frightened creature, a debilitatingly depressed creature, or both by turns. Sometimes, Freud says, the ego actually seeks punishment in the world at the super-ego's behest. In *Civilization and Its Discontents,* he observes that "the tension between the harsh super-ego and the ego that is subjected to it is called by us the sense of guilt; it expresses itself as a need for punishment." When someone possesses an overarching and aching sense of guilt, one way to discharge it is to commit some transgression and suffer punishment for it. Then the super-ego's inflicted guilt disappears—for a while.

Freud suggests that some criminals are more moral than the average person. They are more self-critical and more prone to feeling guilt. A reservoir of self-hatred forms and grows deeper. Then the only thing for the individual to do is to go out and commit a transgression, or perhaps an outright crime, for which the resulting punishment delivers him from his raging super-ego. If the super-ego is fierce enough, and the ego's powers to make it happy are modest, then the charges will begin again and the psychological pain will return. People pass through the world with what we might call a preexisting need for punishment, which the world is often happy to oblige.

Schopenhauer, who may be Freud's most important precursor, says that the will to life is at the center of us all. We are creatures of drives, creatures of appetite. We demand to live, and we want all things that are conducive to living and thriving. Desire brings pain, says Schopenhauer, because it is always based upon a lack, and the not-having hurts. But then, he says, when we satisfy this or that desire, another one or three or six come in, with attendant pain.

So we are creatures who want and who are all too often thwarted in our wanting. But to Schopenhauer's bleak picture we might add another element. We face challenges not only from our desires and the complexities of satisfying them but also from the pressures of the super-ego. We desire and also attack ourselves for desiring. The individual has a couple of tasks to begin with. He must gauge the strength of his desires, but he must also discover the strength of his super-ego. He has to come to some understanding as to whether or not he can live up to its demands—and probably he cannot.

At that point, he must ask himself, What am I supposed to do? How can I navigate life with a potent super-ego, say, and limited powers for satisfying it?

There is also this: according to Freud, with every victory over the ego, the super-ego becomes more demanding, more judgmental, crueler. If an individual is saddled with a sick super-ego, what can she do? If a culture, or an aspect of a culture, is super-ego-ridden, how shall its population respond? If an individual simply wants a better, more productive relationship with his super-ego, is it possible?

Did Freud Discover the Super-Ego?

Freud's thinking about authority and its vicissitudes begins to come into focus in his work during the second decade of the twentieth century. From then on, he is fruitfully obsessed with the question of the super-ego. He enquires into it anthropologically (*Totem and Taboo*); politically (*Group Psychology and the Analysis of the Ego*); therapeutically (in the six famous papers on therapy and technique); and in a strict sense, psychologically (*The Ego and the Id*). He becomes fascinated with authority and its vicissitudes.

Until the midpoint in his career, Freud believes that the task facing every individual is to negotiate and renegotiate his relationship to desire. Through studying desire and its suppression within the ego and in society, the individual has a chance to modulate his own psyche. His destiny, all men's and women's destiny, is to deal with the question of desire and prohibition. But now a third element has entered the equation.

To achieve mental health, the individual has to come to terms with both desire and authority. He needs to temper his own internal agency of prohibition and demand, and he also has to be aware of his relations to authority outside the self. For a pathological relation to the super-ego will almost surely make itself felt in one's encounters with authority figures abroad in the world. Someone whose super-ego is in a state of rage against him may well project that rage onto authority figures in life. He may miss their true intentions because he brings so much preexisting psychological material to the encounter. An enflamed super-ego, one that punishes the individual constantly, may create a level of resentment that the subject cannot but bring into his daily experience. The best name for this activity, Freud thought, is "transference" (*Übertragung*), and there is much to be learned from the concept.

We'll get to that later. Now, let us delve further into the super-ego. Did Freud discover it? Was it always there, waiting to be seen? Or did cultural and historical forces combine to precipitate a new agency in the psyche? Is there something modern about the super-ego?

The idea that conscience could grow ill is anything but new. The Catholic Church was wary of individuals and groups that took the idea of guilt and penance too far, and found it necessary to suppress cults of flagellation and discourage excessive public displays of guilt for one's transgressions. The sacrament of penance is highly ritualized, inward-looking, and subdued. The penitent enters the confessional, confesses sins, and leaves with a sequence of penance. These acts of penance are symbolic. They take the form of prayer. The penitent is asked to "say one Our Father and three Hail Mary's and make a good Act of Contrition." The ceremony can have profound effects, but it takes a muted and predictable form. There will be no raving parades of self-flagellators, at least if the Church has anything to say about it.

The major writer to anticipate Freud's thinking on the matter of conscience gone wrong is, as we saw, the visionary poet William Blake. Like Freud, Blake was given to mapping the inner life. Freud's mappings tend to be fairly straightforward—though the more you read him, the more complex you see them becoming. Ego, id, super-ego: one can start there with a Freudian cartography of the psyche. Blake's inner map is wilder and more changing, but it is not entirely dissimilar.

Urizen, Blake's figure of debased, angry authority, is a drawer of boundaries. As his name suggests, he is prone to creating horizons and is also associated with the rational part of the mind: Urizen suggests "Your Reason." But Urizen's reason is oppressively tyrannical and overbearing. He is an empiricist and insists that everything worth knowing can be known through weights and numbers. How much? How many? He has no time for the soul, no time for the imagination. He is a hater of true poetry and everything that accurately reflects not just the world we live in, but the world we want to live in. He is frozen, a hater of sex, an enemy of freedom of the mind and body. And Blake thinks he rules England, or at least British culture, at the close of the eighteenth century.

Urizen needs to be reformed and redeemed. In what is probably his most accomplished and resolved visionary poem, *Milton,* Blake shows John Milton entering into what Blake would call a "mental fight" with Urizen. Urizen attempts to pour cold water into Milton's brain, baptizing him into the faith of inhumane, cold rationality. But Milton fights back. He scoops up handfuls of wet red clay, the kind that Yahweh used to form Adam, and slaps them on the bony, starved form of Urizen:

> Silent they met, and silent strove among the streams, of
>   Arnon,
> Even to Mahanaim, when with cold hand Urizen stoop'd
>   down
> And took up water from the river Jordan: pouring on
> To Milton's brain the icy fluid from his broad cold palm.
> But Milton took the red clay of Succoth, moulding it with
>   care
> Between his palms; and filling up the furrows of many years
> Beginning at the feet of Urizen, and on the bones
> Creating new flesh on the Demon cold, and, building him
> As with new clay a Human form in the Valley of Beth Peor.

Urizen wants to freeze Milton in this parody of holy baptism, making the poet uncaring and analytical. Milton strives to give Urizen a human form, letting him feel what it is to exist, suffer the world, and enjoy it. He uses red clay, the material the Lord used to form Adam, in an attempt to make Urizen mortal.

The over-I is perhaps a manifestation of the Urizenic wish not to be human, not to be mortal. It wants to live beyond time and perhaps live forever.

Blake's therapy for the sick super-ego is strife—Milton and Urizen engage in a wrestling match, like Jacob and the angel. But it's a humanizing struggle, letting the over-I come down off its fake throne and join the ego as a mere being in the world. Milton slaps red clay on Urizen and makes him a fleshly being who can admit his mortality and enjoy his being righteously. This may be a crude therapy for the demystification of the super-ego, but a therapy it is.

Wrestling the figure of oppression is one solution Blake puts forward. Another is simpler. Blake is deeply devoted to the teachings of Jesus and believes that the savior's essential doctrine comes down to a simple truth: the only way to live fruitfully in the world is by practicing forgiveness. "I forgive you and you forgive me / Together throughout eternity / This our dear redeemer said, / This the wine and this the bread." The sacrament of the Eucharist comes down to one factor—the forgiveness of sins, in oneself and in others. Perhaps it would be possible to make Urizen into a figure of forgiveness; perhaps it would be possible to forgive Urizen as well.

How did the thought of authority gone toxic become available to Blake? Was it always a fact, or a potential fact, of life? Or had social and cultural conditions changed so that a new problem—the modern problem of authority—was emerging in the world?

The Super-Ego's Public History 1: Nietzsche

In a famous passage in *The Gay Science* in which he broods on the death of God, Friedrich Nietzsche suggests that the problem might be something new. To the popular understanding, Nietzsche is the philosopher who claimed we must rid ourselves of God—that God is old-fashioned, a mere superstition, a block on our way to becoming truly free.

Not quite. Nietzsche did not tell the world that it would be a good thing to do away with God but that we had already done so. He looked out on the culture of the nineteenth century not as a prophet but as an observer. God had been done away with, but those who did the deed lacked awareness of what they had done.

They did not know they were living without God. The presence of God, of faith, in daily life had disappeared so gradually, so quietly, that no one saw it happening. Men and women no longer lived with their eyes on the divine; God no longer infused their lives. Thoughts of heaven, thoughts of hell, were at most peripheral to them. God had disappeared and no one had noticed.

And it all seemed natural. It seemed that in the move from a godly culture to a godless one, nothing had changed. Life went on. But in fact, doing away with God was an enormous deed. It would have a deep impact over time. To understand how life would be forever altered, we needed to know what we had done.

In *The Gay Science*, a madman who both is and is not Nietzsche arrives in the marketplace to inform the people that they have committed a momentous act: "The madman jumped into their midst and pierced them with his eyes. 'Whither is God?' he cried; 'I will tell you. *We have killed him*—you and I. All of us are murderers.' And now, what is to be done? 'How shall we comfort ourselves, the murderers of all murderers?' " What kind of funeral observances does the murder of God call for? How shall we mourn the deity? We will need ceremonies of remembrance, to be sure, but what kind? We will need days of collective reflection and perhaps contrition.

How the world has changed since this deed was done. " 'Are we not plunging continually? Backward, sideward, forward, in all directions? Is there still any up or down?' " asks the madman. " 'Are we not straying as through an infinite nothing? Do we not feel the breath of empty space? Has it not become colder? Is not night continually closing in on us? Do we not need to light lanterns in the morning?' " How shall we orient ourselves in this strange world? How shall we find comfort, find meaning?

The madman says we need to deal with our guilt over the most radical deed mankind has ever committed. Surely we will need rituals of forgiveness; surely penance will be required; we will have to admit that we have done the deed and that there is something horrendously vile about it. We did it not only for ourselves but for our children—so they too will feel the effects. Nietzsche wants to know what ablutions we will employ, what days of sorrow we will observe, how we'll confess our sins, how do penance.

He also wonders how we might become worthy of this act. "Is not the greatness of this deed too great for us? Must we ourselves not become gods simply to appear worthy of it?"

At the close of his oration, the madman pauses and looks around. " 'I have come too early,' " he said then; " 'my time is not yet.' " He sees that his audience is in no position to understand, much less assimilate and react to his news. Yet the passage makes one thing clear: humankind's act of killing the deity must in time be reckoned with.

What Nietzsche wants to do, somewhat in the manner of a psychoanalyst, is to make what is unconscious conscious. On some level, we know that we have done away with God, but we have yet to face it in a foursquare way. The madman who is and isn't Nietzsche finds that he has come too early to the marketplace. The crowd assembled has no idea what he's talking about. They chuckle a little because they do not believe in God and see his death as inconsequential. For Nietzsche, it is a cataclysm.

Why does it matter that humanity, or at least Western humanity, takes responsibility for the death of God? Perhaps the best answer is a Freudian one: what is consequential yet unacknowledged in the psyche can come back with redoubled force and distort or even destroy life. If we don't admit to the murder of God, what can happen?

Freud tells us repeatedly and in multiple ways that human beings will never fully abandon a consequential psychological position. They always hold on to it, often through some residue. A man who is in love with a woman, especially if the love has an Oedipal intensity, may lose the woman, but he will continue to pine for her, sometimes for his whole life. And he will seek out substitutes, women who embody some residue of the beloved's qualities. Sylvia Plath dramatizes this sort of displacement in "Daddy," where she says that she lost her father when he died and she was ten (ten in the poem, eight in life), but she never stopped pining for him. She built a model of him, she says, and married it: then she found another man, much like the first, with a "love of the rack and the screw."

Perhaps what happens in the erotic world happens in the world of authority as well. We never completed the death rituals for the God we killed. We never came to terms with the enormity of our deed. We never buried God, or even came close. Would it be so surprising if the deity took up an angry, spiteful residence in our psyches? Suppose that the super-ego is, among other things, the ghost of God? It's all-seeing, all-judging, all-knowing, and brutally retributive, an angry ghost that has never been laid to rest. We are haunted by the worst deed we have ever committed, the murder of God, and his ghost is with us always. To be sure, there are many true believers in the deity in the world. But the more educated segments of the West grow more secular with each generation. And they seem to be the ones most afflicted by the rogue super-ego.

We don't have to stay in Nietzsche's hyperbolic register to see a relation between the fading of God from daily life in the West and the strengthening—or even the creation—of the super-ego. Belief in God and his commandments provided moral stability to men and women. We knew what was true and false, wrong and right. God's ten commandments told us. With the fading of belief, that knowledge faded; for some it disappeared. Maybe the super-ego is a crude replacement for the departed God that manifests itself in the psyche. Salman Rushdie has spoken about a "God shaped hole" in the spirit of modern men and women. Perhaps the super-ego is our effort to fill it.

We might return to Nietzsche's question. Now that the news is abroad and we see and know that we did kill the deity, perhaps we can find a way to placate the departed spirit. Or maybe we should think of it as an exorcism that we need to perform. We need to coax the rogue spirit out of our houses and out of our lives—or at the very least calm it down a little: let it rattle a chain from time to time without controlling our existence. How would such an exorcism be managed? Or to be milder: how could such a calming be achieved?

The Super-Ego's Public History 2: Arendt

"What Is Authority?" is the title of a chapter in Hannah Arendt's *Between Past and Future*. But the question Arendt really wants to ask is, What *was* authority? For authority as she defines it has passed from the modern world. What was it? Why did it decline? Why did it, according to Arendt, disappear?

And then—the question our study compels us to add—what is the relationship between the super-ego and authority? For surely the super-ego traffics in authority. It presumes to know what is good and bad, right and wrong, and is ever-ready to enforce its views on the subject.

Arendt wants us to know exactly what authority is not. It is not coercive power. What the heads of totalitarian states possess cannot be called authority. It's mere force. If you disobey the existing powers you are imprisoned, tortured, maybe killed. True authority does not rely on the fear of harm. Hitler has no authority per se. Mussolini lacks genuine authority. What they possess is merely power.

Nor is authority established through argument and persuasion. Authority, as Arendt understands it, is not a democratic phenomenon. Individuals don't achieve it by staking out a position and then arguing for it well, marshalling facts and drawing the logical conclusions. Authority isn't embodied or achieved by lawyers, journalists, or professors, people who make public their views and then defend them. For Arendt authority is not totalitarian, emerging from all-knowing leaders, and it is not the result of debate in the public sphere. "Authority . . . precludes the use of external means of coercion; where force is used, authority itself has failed. Authority, on the other hand, is incompatible with persuasion, which presupposes equality and works through a process of argumentation. Where arguments are used, authority is left in abeyance."

To Arendt, authority is based upon tradition. We believe what our illustrious ancestors believed, not because it is provable or can be argued for effectively, or because the emperor or dictator says we must. We believe what our ancestors believed for the sole and simple reason that they believed it, and it served them well. We seek to reproduce the thoughts and values of our ancestors and apply them to our own times. A practice or a doctrine is authoritative because it is traditional. It does not need to be proved. Authority is tradition, tradition is authority.

No Western people, according to Arendt, were more committed to authority than the Romans. The Romans were religious—their word *religare* suggests being tied to the past. They were committed to ancestor worship: the gods who dominated the Roman hearth, lares and penates, represented the ancestors. One tried to live up to their high standards, and though one never quite could, one still made the attempt. Shakespeare, who understood far more about Roman culture than many of his critics think, made sure to show how much his Brutus is both inspired and awed by his great ancestor Junius Brutus, who helped to drive the tyrannical Tarquins from Rome. In *Julius Caesar*, Brutus radiates authority not only because of who he is in the present but because of his ties to the past. When he joins the conspiracy, the senators out to kill Caesar have some measure of authority on their side. As Arendt observes, "At the heart of Roman politics, from the beginning of the republic until virtually the end of the imperial era, stands the conviction of the sacredness of foundation, in the sense that once something has been founded it remains binding for all future generations."

Arendt is perhaps thinking of Edmund Burke when she offers her definition of authority. Burke believed in common sense and what he called "prejudice"—a low-church version of Roman authority. Common sense is the day-to-day, ready-to-hand wisdom that has accumulated over time. Those who draw from it, often the poor and the relatively uneducated, may not even be able to say why they do what they do. That's fine with Burke. They are acting wisely in that they are tied to traditional uses. They don't need to be able to defend their best actions and habits—Burke will gladly do that for them—they only need to live them out, secure in the belief that all will be well, or as well as possible. "Prejudice," Burke writes, "is of ready application in the emergency; it previously engages the mind in a steady course of wisdom and virtue, and does not leave the man hesitating at the moment of decision, skeptical, puzzled, and unresolved. Prejudice renders a man's virtue his habit; and not a series of unconnected acts. Through his prejudice, his dignity becomes part of his nature." Prejudice, as Burke uses the word, is founded in authority and comes to us through tradition.

To Burke, traditional knowledge is like a sprawling, sometimes crude, but overall consistent epic poem to which generations of people have contributed. They have added their mite, maybe through a bit of careful revision here and there, but mostly through testing what their parents and priests have taught them and finding it good. In his book on the French Revolution, Burke contrasts this way of life, which he takes to be deeply English, to the way of reckless innovation—which, unsurprisingly, is French.

For good or for ill, what we might call Roman authority is long gone. We no longer want to reproduce the ways of our ancestors, but to improve upon them. We don't accept the word of some individual because he is of a noble or notable family. We have little use for tradition. And the kind of authority that Burke praises seems to be passing from the world.

Today, we ask questions. After the Enlightenment, educated people are not inclined to take truth of any kind on faith—not secular truth and, for many, not religious truth either. The idea that tradition of any sort is always right, or nearly so, is not only untenable, it is absurd, at least among the educated classes. To say that we do things in such and such a way because we did so yesterday and yesteryear appears ridiculous. And this mistrust of authority, this unwillingness to be bound by the past, has had extraordinary results.

The amazing achievements of capitalism, those that Marx and Engels write about in *The Communist Manifesto,* are all around us. Everywhere novelty, everywhere innovation, everywhere fresh theories and fresh ideas. The traditional past is a confinement, an enemy to be overcome. And look at the wonder that capitalism has produced. No one has ever been more in awe of capitalism's achievements than its greatest opponent, Karl Marx.

But something else happens too. "All that is solid melts into air," Marx famously says. Capitalism pulls tradition up by the roots, shakes it once or twice, and then throws it onto the trash heap of the past. Nothing lasts; nothing can be relied upon from one day to the next. Marx describes how the "constant revolutionizing of production, uninterrupted disturbance of all social relations, everlasting uncertainty and agitation, distinguish the bourgeois epoch from all earlier times. All fixed, fast-frozen relationships, with their train of venerable ideas and opinions are swept away, all new-formed ones become obsolete before they can ossify. All that is solid melts into air, all that is holy is profaned, and men at last are forced to face with sober senses the real condition of their lives and their relations with their fellow men." The source of perpetual disruption, disruption of authority included, is the force of capitalism. What Marx attributes to economic forces, Arendt accounts for in political and epistemological terms. Yet they end in the same place: stable authority departs from the modern world.

We need ideas and practices that will help us extract all the wealth from the earth that we possibly can. Then we need ideas that will justify, if only in the most specious terms, what we are doing. Thus there is no end of theories of innovation, of the avant-garde, prizes for innovators and inspired entrepreneurs, celebrations of the future and degradations of tradition.

A crisis of authority: that is what Arendt sees in the modern world. When you devalue tradition and find your truth by way of open argument (if you are lucky) or encounter it through coercion and propaganda (if you are not), you've lost contact with authority. To which someone might say, "All to the good." We don't need authority, it's a conservative trap that keeps the rich rich, the poor poor, and the ignorant exactly where they were yesterday. Hurrah for positive science. Hurrah for truth argued for and argued for again. And all this may have its bearing.

But for many, the departure of authority from the world will be destabilizing. It's not only that the center no longer holds but that there's no more center. The experience Marx describes, in which all that's solid melts into air, is perhaps liberating for the confident, the aggressive, and the adventurous. But for others, when it all melts away, what are we left with but the amazing whirr of time that never stops? As Arendt says, "Authority, resting on its foundation in the past as its unshakeable cornerstone, gave the world the permanence and durability which human beings need precisely because they are mortals—the most unstable and futile beings we know of. Its loss is tantamount to the loss of the groundwork of the world, which indeed since then has begun to shift, to change and transform itself with ever-increasing rapidity from one shape into another, as though we were living and struggling with a Protean universe where everything at any moment can become almost anything else."

Wouldn't people who have been deracinated by the departure of authority and by Marx's melting find themselves hungry for some substitute authority? Might they not have a place in their psyches for a force that appears to dispense eternal if overly simple truths? Unable to enjoy actual authority, might they not be all too open to authority's corrupted ghost?

Rushdie, as I've said, finds a "God-shaped hole" in all of us. Maybe the hole is shaped like God (as Nietzsche's thought suggests), but maybe it is a space that yearns for any sort of authority, any sort of tradition. And then—maybe—enter the super-ego. The super-ego is, among other things, a residue of the past, modeled in part on the parents' sense of prohibition. Thus it has some continuity with a prior state, with a past, even though it is not a collective and publicly approved past. When public authority disappears, one may be left with the familial authority. While such authority may be potent, it is a residue of the childhood past and not fit for the grown man or woman. The problem is that as the individual matures, modern society offers nothing—no conception of God, no Roman-like authority—with which to replace it. So the super-ego stays as it is: undeveloped, uneducated, unredeemed.

In different ways, both Arendt and Nietzsche point toward a crisis of authority. Nietzsche describes the death of religious authority; Arendt, the death of authority in the public world. The two writers are compatible: one sees the failure of faith, the other the failure of stabilizing political order. The main point is that most human beings need authority. We need some direction from culture and religion to live stably and satisfyingly in the world. When legitimate forms of authority disappear, the way is open for rogue authority to assert itself. When there is nothing reliable outside you to help you organize your life, internal forces enter the empty space, and those forces may be anything but benevolent. In the outside world, on comes the dictator; on comes the religious huckster. The conditions that Nietzsche and Arendt describe did not create the super-ego. That involves another dynamic. But the crises of authority, religious and secular, do leave a space for inner, regressive authority to expand and expand and never be cultivated or displaced.

The Personal History of the Super-Ego

Freud's theory about the inception of the super-ego is harsh and, for many, difficult to believe. But it would be wrong to skip past it. Readers must judge for themselves. Does it take an event as violent (and grotesque) as the one Freud describes to implant super-ego authority in the child? Or is it the case, as I believe it is, that parental prohibitions, social pressures, and the absence or attenuation of legitimate public authority and religious authority are enough to install the super-ego and invest it with energy?

How does the super-ego get started in a human being? Freud's story about the origins of the super-ego is intimate, familial. The super-ego, he famously said, is the heir to the Oedipal complex. Before what Freud calls the Oedipal passage, the child does not possess a super-ego. It's the shock and fear, fear of the father, that precipitates the Oedipal passage in the child. The shock is based on the delivery of a furious prohibition and a threat.

Freud issued the theory of the Oedipal complex in his first major book, *The Interpretation of Dreams,* published in 1899 but dated 1900 to reflect Freud's view that his book would inaugurate a new century. The contours of the complex are well known. The child, early in life, is possessed by desire for the mother. Whether male or female, the child wants to own its mother exclusively. And in time, it becomes clear that exclusive possession of the mother involves doing away with the father. To fulfill his greatest wish, or hers, the father must go.

At a critical point, the father, on whatever level of consciousness, sees what the child wants and makes the actual facts of the situation completely clear. I alone possess mother: he generally does not say as much but signifies it. He indicates to the child that henceforth, clinging, clutching, erotic kissing, and erotic embrace are forbidden. But he goes further. To the male child, he issues what Freud calls the castration threat. If the child does not squelch his desire for mother, he will lose his most precious organ. The father will do away with it.

The shock of this threat is overwhelming. The male child violently represses his desire for the mother and disowns sexuality altogether. He will not return to sexual life until the hormonal charge delivered at puberty overwhelms his inhibitions and he becomes actively desiring again. Meanwhile, he enters a latency phase in which sexual desire exists in him but is fully repressed. This is the period we associate with childhood innocence, though another term for it might be "traumatic fear."

The father's threat establishes the basis of the new interior agency, the super-ego. Its nature is in large part determined by its origins, which are sudden, violent, and, from the child's point of view, crude. Henceforth a residue of that experience will remain with the individual, and it will be at the heart of the super-ego's identity. The child will grow up to be a creature of fear and shame.

Freud sees the young girl as traveling a slightly different path. She too desires the mother; she too stimulates the father's jealousy; she too receives a prohibition. But it is not nearly as fierce as the one the boy encounters. Castration can't be at issue here. So there is no threat, delivered or imagined. Instead the father disparages the girl. She cannot possibly possess the mother because she lacks the equipment to do so. She's incomplete, and accordingly will never amount to much in the world. There is little hope for her. Henceforth, according to Freud, she often experiences her life as based on lack and inadequacy.

But because it is more mildly and subtly installed, her super-ego is not as fierce and punitive as the boy's. It's more lenient, more allowing. She doesn't have the ferocious super-ego presence her brother does, because hers is based on an insult—an intimate and devastating insult to be sure, but not a threat of traumatic violence.

The super-ego, strong or mild, radically punitive or moderately so, is the heir to the Oedipal complex. Or so Freud insists. I'm not sure he is right. It seems to me that cultural pressures for obedience and conformity are probably sufficient to establish what amounts to an agency within the psyche, an unwelcome guest in the realm of the self. As the Ralph Waldo Emerson of "Self-Reliance" attests in so many ways, one can readily see society as a "joint-stock company, in which the members agree, for the better securing of his bread to each shareholder, to surrender the liberty and culture of the eater. The virtue in most request is conformity. Self-reliance is its aversion. It loves not realities and creators, but names and customs." So a potent (and pernicious) society could readily, it seems to me, install voices and values into the soul of the individual. There may be something to Freud's Gothic horror story about how pernicious authority takes its place in the individual. But as society and socialization have grown more potent, it makes sense to seek the origin of the super-ego in culture. In the long run, how the over-I originates may not matter. However it begins, the objective remains the same: to understand and revise this agency that can do us, and the culture, so much harm.

The Future of the Super-Ego

Freud is not generally a historicist. He tends to be what writers a few decades ago would have called an "essentialist." He believes there is something we can justly call "human nature." He believes that with the help of previous writers like Shakespeare and Dostoyevsky, and by way of his own observations in therapy and in life, he has come close to understanding it. We are all still children, we are all still primitive people, according to Freud: and between children and primitive people, he sees little difference.

To this dramatic affirmation of a more or less stable human nature, there is one major exception in Freud's work. This is his theory of the super-ego. In what now may be his only commonly read book, *Civilization and Its Discontents*, he puts forward fresh thoughts about the super-ego, and they are at least implicitly evolutionary.

Civilization, by which Freud means social organization and technological and scientific development, is growing more potent. It delivers us ever more security, safety, comfort, ease, and health, and there is every chance that this will continue. Is this a good thing? By and large, Freud thinks it is. Better to be reasonably prosperous and in good enough health than not. He does complain that civilization causes some of the ills that it then seeks to cure. We have high-speed trains, Freud says, and that's a good thing. But I wouldn't need a high-speed train to go and visit my daughter if she had stayed close to home, as she probably would have done in an era before reliable transportation and mobile culture. But this is a cavil and he knows it. Overall, technology and medical advances please him.

What doesn't please him is the dynamic relationship between the super-ego and civilization. The book's relevant thesis is simple: as civilization develops, the super-ego grows stronger. And it may happen, one might infer, that the super-ego will grow so strong that life under its reign will not be worth living. The book is almost entirely pessimistic. Its perceptions are tragic. Our highest achievement, civilization, is making us sick and might in time lead to our destruction. Unbridled id—rampant desire—can destroy a civilization; that's plain. But Freud proposes that an unbridled moral or supra-moral force could do so as well. In "Fire and Ice," Robert Frost broods on the end of the world: will it end in fire or in ice? He says that from what he knows of desire, he "holds with those who favor fire":

> But if it has to perish twice,
> I think I know enough of hate
> To say that for destruction ice
> Is also great
> And would suffice.

We may fall to unbridled desire; we may also fall to colder, more insidious forms of hatred, including self-hatred.

Friedrich Hegel said that tragedy occurs when two consequential goods collide with each other. His paradigmatic example is Sophocles' *Antigone,* which pits the rights of the individual and the family against the demands of the state. Antigone wants to bury her brother, Polynices, with due honor. Creon, the king, believes he was a disloyal rebel and orders his body left to rot in the fields. The welfare of individuals and the family conflict with the needs to the state. Both elements, family and state, are humanly necessary and often admirable. Their collision creates a tragedy. For Freud, the two elements at play are civilization and the individual. The development of nonviolent, protective civilization is a great good, but so too is the individual's right to tranquility of spirit.

The super-ego inhibits not only erotic desire but also aggression. As society becomes less and less tolerant of violent or even self-assertive behavior—as a middle-class society almost inevitably does—more and more of the aggressive energy that comes with being human must be suppressed. This makes entire sense—everyone knows as much or could infer it.

But then comes the critical question: what happens to the aggressive energy that we would like to discharge externally but cannot? Freud has a direct answer: it is taken up by the super-ego. The super-ego appropriates the force that, if discharged into the world, would bring harm to others and later to the subject himself. So the super-ego takes over that aggressive energy and, as is its wont, discharges it against the ego. The more the subject says no to aggression, the more power the super-ego accrues. "The effect of instinctual renunciation on the conscience," says Freud, "is that every piece of aggression the subject gives up is taken over by the super-ego and increases the latter's aggressiveness (against the ego)."

And society advances, Freud tells us, by compelling us to become ever more civilized. We think our city is truly civilized when we can walk confidently down the streets at night; when the government uses persuasion, not violence, for its ends; and when people discuss rather than argue, argue rather than fight, and—last resort—throw a punch rather than reach for a weapon. So life becomes more secure, but we also become more bottled up—and our inner enemy, the super-ego, grows in strength.

Some of us, Freud avers, can take our aggressive energy and transform it. We channel it into scientific research; we use it for art; we employ it to start and sustain a business. This transformation of aggression into energies that contribute to the betterment of society and culture is what Freud calls sublimation. And it is a wonderful solution to civilization's dilemma. You take potentially destructive forces and turn them to constructive purposes. You bring good to others and even gather rewards for it. Perfect, no?

Yet there's a problem. (In the psychoanalytical consideration of life, there is always a problem.) The difficulty is that very few people are capable of sustained acts of sublimation. We simply cannot do it. We cannot rechannel our rogue energies into productive pursuits, at least in a protracted, consistent way. We are creatures of instinct who demand primary satisfaction, and when we cannot get it, we rebel. The super-ego quells our rebellion by undermining the ego, and the ego's desires to behave overboldly. Most of us do not possess enough discipline, education, and talent to take the route of sublimation, and even those who do usually can't sustain their efforts consistently.

Freud notes that the intensity of sublimated activities "is mild as compared with the sating of crude and primary instinctual impulses; it does not convulse our physical being. And the weak point of this method is that it is not applicable generally: it is accessible to only a few people. It presupposes the possession of special dispositions and gifts which are far from being common to any practical degree. And even to the few who do possess them, this method cannot give complete protection from suffering. It creates no impenetrable armor against the arrows of fortune, and it habitually fails when the source of suffering is the person's own body."

As society demands more and more disavowal of our instincts, the super-ego grows stronger. Society becomes a superficially more agreeable place—it is certainly more peaceful; life is better assured. But the individual is in no position to take full satisfaction in these developments because he lives with the oppressions—anxiety, despondency, neuroses—visited upon him by the super-ego.

In *Civilization and Its Discontents,* Freud speaks of the "cultural super-ego" in describing the way cultural prohibitions echo and augment the super-ego of the individual. So now the super-ego has its own culture. Is there any alternative culture, any counterculture to the super-ego's reign of punishment and guilt-creation? Says Freud, "if the development of civilization has such a far-reaching similarity to the development of the individual and if it employs the same methods, may we not be justified in reaching the diagnosis that, under the influence of cultural urges, some civilizations, or some epochs of civilization—possibly the whole of mankind—have become neurotic?"

As civilization develops, the rule of the super-ego gets tighter, and it will continue to do so, Freud indicates, unless something is done. Perhaps it is truly possible: an epoch can become neurotic.

Super-Ego Dreams

Freud began his career as a psychoanalytical writer with *The Interpretation of Dreams*. He thought it would inaugurate the new century, but it did nothing of the kind. Virtually no one read it; virtually no one reviewed it. In time it became a classic work, and perhaps it did help define the twentieth century. At first, however, there was almost no interest in Freud's dream book. But it did get him moving: it was a basis of his thinking for the next forty years. In the book, he describes the life of the unconscious mind, offers a map of the psyche (without the super-ego), and propounds a theory of dreams.

A dream, he taught, is the disguised fulfillment of a repressed wish. The conscious mind will not abide the presence of certain forbidden desires, Oedipal ones chiefly, and it suppresses them during daylight hours. At night, our wishes can express themselves, but in coded, symbolic form. Thus dreams require interpretation.

Freud looked back on the book with no little pride. He said that insights of such magnitude come to a person only once in a lifetime. In his later life he revised only two of his books. One was the dream book, the other his early book *Three Essays on the Theory of Sexuality*, which includes his highly controversial piece on infantile eros. He added passages, made corrections, and entered footnotes, multiplying versions of *The Interpretation of Dreams* as the years went by. Change it as he might, he never forgot the book's fundamental argument: a dream is a disguised fulfillment of a repressed wish. Desire is at the center of the book, and it remains so through every revision.

What about bad dreams? What about anxious and guilty dreams, dreams of pursuit, dreams of oppression? Those, Freud says, are often more deeply encoded than the rest. They use anxiety and fear to cover over the authentic desire at their cores. In Freud's dream theory, the wish is always preeminent. A dream is the fulfillment—indirect and disguised by the dream work—of a wish, the representation of an unconscious desire.

Freud changed his mind about the structure of the psyche fifteen years later. Now there's a super-ego, and it is often unconscious. But he never carried his new thoughts about the over-I into his dream theory. Can there not now be super-ego dreams? Can't one reasonably say that dreams come in two sorts? One is desire-based dreams, the other dreams based in judgment. All of our Kafkaesque dreams—appearing before an implacable judge; being imprisoned without cause; being the person against whom all hands are raised—might be considered emanations from the super-ego. The Greeks believed that dreams came from two sources: the gates of horn and the gates of ivory. Dreams from the ivory gate are false; dreams from the horn gate, true.

Perhaps our dreams also come from two sources, id and super-ego. Both are in large measure unconscious, and thus hard to read and interpret with the waking mind. Dreams, Freud said, are the royal road to the unconscious. He meant the unconscious id, of course. But why not the unconscious super-ego as well? Perhaps the super-ego encodes its messages in the same complex and distorting idiom that the id does. Perhaps there are super-ego dreams that also can be interpreted.

Why does this matter? We learned to hear the voice of unsanctioned and forbidden desire through the analysis of dreams, without which our true desires are difficult to make contact with. And to Freud, that contact is crucial. Even if we do not act on a forbidden desire, knowing about it can give us some tranquility of mind. To Freud, desire wishes to be known, wishes to speak its name. When that happens and the subject, sometimes with the aid of an analyst, can understand and accept the desire, anxiety and turbulence are reduced. We know better what we are dealing with, and even our hidden desires become things we can acknowledge, accept, maybe even joke about. One thinks of Peter Gay's great line: Freud taught us that there is more to understand and less to judge about human behavior than we have previously supposed.

Before Freud, we did not know quite who we were—according to Freud. He helped us know ourselves through the medium of desire. Then he told us that that our relations to authority were as defining as our relations to desire, and made the case in some detail. But the over-I, like the id, is unconscious, and Freud did not mark out many strategies for getting to know the over-I in its particularity. He did not teach us how to communicate with the super-ego, or how it could communicate with us.

A new dream book is needed, from which we may learn to decode the oneiric language of the over-I. If dreams are the royal roads to the unconscious id, they may also be a royal road to the unconscious over-I.

Says Freud, the super-ego asserts itself "through the medium of the voice." But it is a voice we rarely hear or are attuned to hearing. In dreams, we might be able to begin to listen to that voice—dreams, at least mine, do have an audible dimension. By so hearing, we might learn about who and what we are, and find ourselves, as Wallace Stevens puts it, "more truly and more strange." Perhaps we could do more than hear the haunting voice of the super-ego. Maybe we could enter into dialogue with it, and in that dialogue between ego and super-ego, begin to know ourselves and to lose some of our needless sorrow. But this is a matter we shall take up later.

The Post-Modern Super-Ego

Many thinkers who came after Freud recognized that there is something wrong with our relations to authority. Some adopted a direct version of Freud's super-ego. Others renamed the agency and redefined it after their own fashion.

Among the most prominent and original of these is Michel Foucault. Foucault's interest is in power and discipline, most saliently discipline. Michael Walzer describes Foucault's work as like an extended pun on the word *discipline*. Foucault is interested in the way society breeds and enforces conformity—how a culture gets its citizens to stay in line.

This happens through the promulgation of disciplines, particularly academic and institutional disciplines. All of the disciplines that define and seek to understand human beings create limits, usually stultifying ones. Disciplines oppress through that process of normalization. Psychology, which Foucault particularly detests, provides not only defining diagnoses but also an array of psychological types. The therapeutic world applies these types in its own sphere, but also disseminates them into the culture at large, into schools, prisons, clinics, and even churches. Once we are defined, we are in a position to be disciplined. Through institutionally endorsed and enforced disciplines, our lives are constricted.

The disciplines of the human sciences—psychology, sociology, criminology, anthropology, medicine, and more—are taken up by institutions like schools and the military, which apply and enforce them. At a certain point in life, you take an I.Q. test. This test derives from the discipline of psychology, but it has effects in the world. Your teachers, counselors, and maybe even your parents use your score to create a version of you and what your possibilities are. Then, in some measure, they enforce that sense by funneling you into the "appropriate classes"; steering you to the "correct" sort of job; and treating you with more or less respect and consideration based upon your results. The discipline of metrical psychology, apparently detached and objective, manifests itself in the world of experience, especially institutional experience, and helps draw defining disciplinary boundaries for the individual, which confine his or her possibilities.

Disciplines discipline.

This is especially true, Foucault thinks, of the discourse on sex. He resists the current impulse to define people by their sexual proclivities. He would, I think, endorse an observation of Gore Vidal's: There are homosexual acts, yes. But there are no homosexual persons. The culture offers descriptions of various types and then enforces those descriptions in subtle and unsubtle ways. A disciplinary society needs there to be homosexual persons, the better to control them and encourage them to control themselves.

Disciplinary society does its work through surveillance and authoritative description, and in so doing, it limits human possibility. The implication of Foucault's work is that we internalize our disciplinary identities and they oppress us through the mechanisms of our institutions, cutting off further possibilities and pleasures. His view of authority responds to the workings of an ever more comprehensive bureaucratic society. He would no doubt have seen the Internet's capacity to breed conformity through its powers of regulation, observation, and quantification as a very successful extension of existing disciplinary society.

The emblem of Foucault's version of toxic authority is the panopticon, a prison design created by Jeremy Bentham. The inmates in the panoptic prison, which was never actually built, can be seen at any time of the day or night by their keepers. But the prisoners have no idea when they are being watched and when they are not. They cannot see either their observers or their fellow inmates. They begin to behave as though the keepers are watching all the time, whether they are or not, and internalize the prison's standards for comportment. In so doing, they become subjects of a surveillance that, at any given moment, may not be occurring. It may not have been happening for weeks and even months, but they proceed as though it is. Freud might say that they internalize a panoptic super-ego. Foucault puts it this way: "Hence the major effect of the Panopticon: to induce in the inmate a state of consciousness and permanent visibility that assures the automatic functioning of power. So to arrange things that the surveillance is permanent in its effects, even if it is discontinuous in its action; that the perfection of power should tend to render its actual exercise unnecessary; that this architectural apparatus should be a machine for creating and sustaining a power relation independent of the person who exercises it; in short, that the inmates should be caught up in a power situation of which they are themselves the bearers." Thus the prisoners become principals of their own subjection.

In a society based upon discipline and surveillance, Foucault implies, we are not unlike prisoners in the panopticon, in that though we may not always be under surveillance, we continue to comport ourselves as though we were. We subscribe to the disciplinary ethos when we are under its direct control, in school or at work, and also when we are physically apart from the apparatus of discipline. *They* may be surreptitiously watching—the technology is very advanced. But more likely, *we* are watching ourselves on their behalf, monitoring our behavior as though the authorities were in the room with us. They have become us; we become them.

They? Not quite. Foucault suggests that there is no "they." His analysis has little to do with Orwell-style social oppression, in that for Foucault there is no Party as in *1984*, and no elevated class (no pigs) as in *Animal Farm*. Surveillance and discipline take on a life of their own, wherever there are resources to support them. They function in no one's behalf and achieve no advantage for any party, sect, or class. Discipline has a life all its own, far more durable and resistant than what might be imposed by even the most potent political party or ruling clique. Discipline only seeks its own development and deployment, and it does so with no end in mind. We are discipline, discipline is us.

To this what does Freud have to say? Surely he would be pleased with Foucault's focus on authority, and on rogue authority in particular. He might admit that the kind of disciplinary surveillance that was abroad when Foucault wrote was rather different from that of his own time. So Foucault's work would qualify as an advance on Freud's construction of the *cultural super-ego*. I think Freud would likely be most grateful. At the same time, he would be reluctant to locate the ultimate origin of current toxic authority exclusively in society and outside the family.

Yet in Foucault we encounter a vision of discipline, both intellectual and institutional, as it has developed since Freud's lifetime and has done remarkable work to strength the kingdom of the over-I.

Death and the Super-Ego

"The aim of all life is death," Freud notoriously said. But all of us have an urge to die in our own particular way.

Freud introduced the idea of the Death Drive late in his career, claiming that it is an absolutely independent instinct that inhabits humans and maybe all life. The Death Drive is simply the hunger to pass away, slough off the mortal coil, and leave the world. But we wish to do it after our own fashion, and often we contrive to do precisely that. But we also do all we can to refuse to perish in any way but our own. The instinct of life, Eros, opposes the Death Drive.

Where does the Death Drive come from? It is an elemental force in humans that is "beyond the pleasure principle." It motivates behavior that aims at harming the self or wreaking destruction on the world. It is the antithesis of the instinct for life that Freud at times champions. Yet he cannot find a plausible origin for the Death Drive.

Freud makes his first extended argument for the Drive in the 1920 volume *Beyond the Pleasure Principle*. There he points to a number of human behaviors that do not seem to serve the pleasure principle but have darker, more destructive motives. Among those behaviors is the human tendency to repeat traumatic events, bringing them up into the conscious mind and playing them through. There cannot be any pleasure in remembering pain, Freud says, especially when the pain is of an intimate sort. Yet he also suggests that repetition may be a way of slowly coming to terms with and finally accepting past pain. In the fashion commended by Nietzsche, we might be turning "Thus it was into Thus I willed it," thereby shedding our status as victims. For every proposed instance of the exertion of the Death Drive in *Beyond the Pleasure Principle,* there seems to be an explanation that can bring the event back under the reign of the principle of pleasure. In an intricately argued essay on the book, Jacques Derrida shows that everything comes back under the domain of *le pépé,* Derrida's name for both the principle of pleasure and for Freud, the grandfather, the pépé, who begins his enquiry by investigating a repeating game, fort / da, played by his grandson. The pleasure principle and the authority of Freud, founder of psychoanalysis, win out all through the book.

In thinking about the Death Drive, Freud had an obvious theoretical recourse. What could the drive be but the ultimate expression of the over-I's rage against the I? At a certain point, guilt becomes so strong, Freud had argued before, that it takes us to suicide. This is a central argument of his brilliant paper on loss and death, "Mourning and Melancholia." We feel the pressure of the super-ego, he writes; then we go out and transgress so as to be punished to satisfy the irrational guilt we carry with us. One has behaved badly and can find no way to discharge the guilt. There is no religious or secular ritual that can restore to us the feeling of relative innocence. So we commit a reckless crime, get caught, pay their penalty, and emerge cleansed—at least temporarily.

What is the ultimate self-punishment if not death? The badly tortured soul must find a way to be cleansed. And there are some crimes—or perceptions of crime—that no human punishment can absolve. What then to do? Suicide is surely a possibility. But much psychological life goes on underground, in the unconscious. We seek without knowing what we are seeking, or why. We find punishment for crimes we do not know we have committed, and find it in disproportion to those crimes. We seek punishment, and when no punishment that will keep us on earth is enough, we may seek death. There, I think, is a version of the Death Drive that does not defy belief.

Freud glances in this direction at least once in his career. In *The Ego and the Id,* he discusses melancholia, a stubborn, bitter condition defined by anxiety and self-hatred. "Following our view of sadism," he says, "we should say that the destructive component had entrenched itself in the super-ego and turned against the ego. What is now holding sway in the ego is, as it were, a pure culture of the death instinct, and in fact it often enough succeeds in driving the ego into death, if the latter does not fend off its tyrant in time by the change round into mania."

Why did Freud not adopt this view overall? Surely it occurred to him. Lionel Trilling has suggested that Freud wanted to affirm a part of human life that culture could not touch. The Death Drive comes before socialization and lives past it too. Freud, beset by cancer and by his vision of the world of the 1920s beginning to tear itself apart, may have been grappling with his own wish to leave the world.

Perhaps he wished to die in his own fashion—and that fashion was cancer. He did not bother to find treatment for it until very, very late. By the time he showed his abscessed jaw to his physician, the cancer was already highly advanced. He took no pain-killer stronger than aspirin, wishing at all times to keep his mind clear for work. He endured over thirty operations for the cancer, and when he felt he had suffered enough, he let his physician know it was time to end it. He died, he might have said, in collaboration with the Death Drive as he conceived it. He recognized it, honored it, and affirmed it to the last.

Yet the reasons for connecting the over-I and the Death Drive are manifold. The wonder is why Freud did not accept them.

PART TWO
Super-Ego Culture

Politics and the Super-Ego 1: Hypnotized!

Can the super-ego—call it the cultural super-ego if you like—take possession of political life?

Freud spent the second half of his career brooding on the question of authority, which is inseparable from the question of the super-ego. And he considered the political issue. In *Group Psychology and the Analysis of the Ego*, he took up the subject of crowds and groups, how they come into being, and how they behave once they're composed. He begins by reflecting on the work of Gustav le Bon, who sees groups as regressive formations that take the individual back to a more primal, less thoughtful condition. Le Bon is interested in the group mind and how it frees the subject from the burden of individual thinking. In most groups, Le Bon sees certain features: "the weakness of intellectual ability, the lack of emotional restraint, the incapacity for moderation and delay, the inclination to exceed every limit in the expression of emotion and to work it off completely in the form of action."

Freud concurs overall about the regressive tendency of groups, but he has something to add. To Freud, Le Bon fails to see the fundamental nature of groups because he does not address the ultimate question, the question of the leader. In Freud's view, masses don't come together and create a group mind; they're brought together by the energies of a primary figure. Occasionally groups coalesce under a leader with good results. Productive work gets done; crises are met and managed. But for the most part, groups are regressive. They form under a leader, and the leader takes them toward thoughtless, often destructive action.

Freud has a clear sense of what makes someone a leader, especially the leader of a destructive group. The leader type appears to be absolutely self-reliant and self-contained. He (and it almost always is a he) loves no one but himself, though he is able to dispense the illusion that he loves every member of his group equally. He presents a masterful front—nothing daunts him. He's a figure of absolute knowledge, never wrong, always ahead of the crowd (but not too far). He may mock others, but he never mocks or criticizes himself. He never says, "I was wrong," not only because it is not in his nature to do so but because his followers do not wish to hear it. Freud compares the modern leader to the head of the prehistoric group he calls the "primal horde": "His intellectual acts were strong and independent, even in isolation, and his will needed no reinforcement from others. Consistency leads us to assume that his ego had few libidinal ties; he loved no one but himself, or other people only insofar as they served his needs. To objects his ego gave away no more than was barely necessary."

Freud's book is prophetic. It describes a span of twentieth- and twenty-first-century leaders: Hitler, Mao, Lenin, Stalin, Pol Pot, and more. For whatever complex of reasons, people have been willing to surrender their free will and put themselves in the hands of man-gods. Some have not gone along, but in certain nations, at certain times, the great majority has. And they continue to do so. The 45th American president did not have the power of last century's dictators, but he possesses many of their temperamental attributes. He is oppressively self-confident, ever-boastful, never admits error, and lacks all sense of humor, especially about himself. He is, to his own mind, never wrong, and never has been. His followers often regard him with something like the awe that Germans and Russians brought to their own demigods. "I alone can save us," he has said, and many have apparently concurred.

The leader, Freud says, effectively *hypnotizes* the members of the group. He puts them in a trance and gives them assurance, direction, and the illusion of stability. But in return they give up their free will. During hypnotism, says Freud, the hypnotist puts the ego at least partially to sleep. He enchants it, makes it slightly drunk. What's left is the part of the self that Freud associates with "primary process." He makes the subject a little high, relieving the subject of the burden of reason and bringing him closer to his spontaneous self. Some of us, as all hypnotists know, are more readily put under hypnosis than others. Some people get very sleepy, very sleepy, very sleepy as the hypnotist chants in his lulling voice. And then they are ready to stand up on stage, wiggle like snakes, waddle like ducks, and all the rest. They are, presumably, people who are singularly willing to get rid of the burden of independent thought and transfer it to someone else

Transferring reason and judgment to another is the essence of hypnotism, Freud says, and also the essence of crowd behavior. We want to get rid of intellection. We want to shed the responsibility of making our way through a complex world. The leader tells us it is all very simple. It's something that he, and he only, can understand. So hand over your will and intelligence and let him lead the way; become a willing subject. Says Freud: "The hypnotic relation is the unlimited devotion of someone in love, but with sexual satisfaction excluded."

Hypnotism and crowd behavior rely on a splitting of the psyche. The subject transfers a part of himself to the hypnotist and becomes a partial being, less thoughtful, less free, and less mature than he was. What happens in a regressive group is quite clear to Freud: the individual puts the leader in the place of the super-ego. What advantage does the subject gain by doing so? His own super-ego may be variable, strange, difficult to please. But here in front of him is one that is clear and precise in what he values. The transference of the super-ego to an external being stabilizes the self. Now we know what to love and value.

Super-ego transference also confers security. The super-ego is based in certain ways on the father, and as Freud often tells us, we spend much of our lives pining for the return of the father's authority. We never willingly surrender a libidinal position, he says, and one of the most satisfying of all such positions is the relation we sustain with our fathers when we are small and need their protection. We return to that when we immerse ourselves in the crowd and submit our will to the will of the leader.

The leader makes the super-ego external, Freud says, by embodying it himself. And the leader does something else as well: he changes the nature of the super-ego, at least temporarily. A productive leader may do this in useful ways. A Churchill, a Roosevelt, a Lincoln may ask people to surpass themselves in their commitment to a worthwhile cause. They ask reasonably, give or take, and they ask for contributions the individual can deliver, though sometimes with difficulty. Yet such transference of authority is productive overall.

But there is another, obscene form of super-ego transference. In it, the leader embodies authority, but he uses it to promote cruelty, hatred, crime. He gives the stamp of his authority to the least admirable human urges. In his persona, he blends super-ego and id. He gives his followers the satisfactions of authority but also, sometimes almost surreptitiously, gives them permission to indulge their worst impulses. Getting the mix of apparently constructive authority and attendant cruelty just right is the achievement, if one may call it that, of the deeply pernicious dictators.

One sees it in the most destructive form in Hitler, who spoke about the need to sacrifice for the glory of Germany. He was patriotic; he enjoined love of country. He praised the high ideals of the German people. But at the same time, he encouraged the Germans to rob and murder their Jewish neighbors. This blending of high ideals with demonic license is one of the most dangerous political conjunctions the world knows. You saw intimations of it in the 45th president's claims of patriotism, his purported love for America and wish to make it great again. He wanted, he said, to help his country reach the highest of ideals. Yet at the same time, he insulted Latin Americans, women, Blacks, and immigrants, and opened the door to violence against them. He blended the authoritative—"I alone can save us"—with the subversively cruel. And virtually all of us, both supporters and detractors, find him mesmerizing. (The kind of hatred that 45's detractors feel for him is not the reverse of love, Freud would tell us. Indifference is. In ongoing hatred, there is a tribute, a flattering fascination.) As Richard Sennett says in *Authority,* "The dilemma of authority in our time, the peculiar fear it inspires, is that *we feel attracted to strong figures that we do not feel to be legitimate.*"

Stephen Greenblatt compares 45's mesmerizing power to that of Shakespeare's Richard III. "What excites him," Greenblatt says of Richard, "is the joy of domination. He is a bully. Easily enraged, he strikes out at anyone who stands in his way. He enjoys seeing others cringe, tremble or wince with pain. He is gifted at detecting weakness, and gifted at mockery and insult. These skills attract followers who are drawn to the same cruel delight, even if they cannot have it to his unmatched degree."

But it's not only Richard's followers who are drawn to him. He mesmerizes the audience too. "There are," Greenblatt says, "those who take vicarious pleasure in the release of pent-up aggression, in the black humor of it all, in the open speaking of the unspeakable. . . . It is not necessary to look around to find people who embody this category of collaborators. They are we, the audience, charmed again and again by the villain's jaunty outrageousness, by his indifference to the ordinary norms of human decency, by the lies that seem to be effective even though no one believes them, by the seductive power of sheer ugliness. Something in us enjoys every minute of this horrible ascent to power." What we are responding to, I think, is the sight of a figure of surpassing authority, a super-ego figure, embodying and encouraging the worst sort of crime.

Donald Trump is no Hitler, nor is he on a par with Shakespeare's Richard III. But he combines some of their qualities to create an intoxicating brew. And of course it intoxicates not only those who are smitten with Trump but also his many, often highly articulate detractors. They too are fascinated by his combination of authority and depravity, and their willingness—even need—to spend so many hours reiterating their loathing for Trump is a phenomenon worthy of explication.

Were they themselves somehow tempted by this blending of license and ostensibly high-minded authority? Would they like to enjoy it for themselves? Perhaps what they want is a way to live from the super-ego and the id, without the inconvenience of the thoughtful, sanely judging self. Maybe it is every child's dream to do exactly what he likes, indulging all appetites, and to rule from on high and think surpassingly well of himself in the bargain.

In *Achieving Our Country*, published in 1997, Richard Rorty effectively predicted political events twenty years down the line. Rorty looks ahead to a time when "members of labor unions, and unorganized unskilled workers, will . . . realize that their government is not even trying to prevent wages from sinking or to prevent jobs from being exported. Around the same time, they will realize that suburban white collar workers—themselves desperately afraid of being downsized—are not going to let themselves be taxed to provide social benefits for anyone else." Surely it would not be reckless to say that all this has come to pass. "At this point something will crack,"

Rorty writes. "The nonsuburban electorate will decide that the system has failed and start looking around for a strongman to vote for—someone willing to assure them that, once he is elected, the smug bureaucrats, tricky lawyers, overpaid bond salesmen, and post-modern professors will no longer be calling the shots."

This is brilliantly prophetic, as far as it goes. I can think of no better compressed version of what has occurred in American politics over the last couple of decades. What Freud adds to Rorty's account is the psychological dimension. The strongman that Rorty describes appeals to a major component of his adherents' inner lives (and maybe those of his detractors). He is a surrogate super-ego, whose power is not only political but emotional—and this is why he (and those who may come after him) will be so hard to defend against and finally to displace. Commentators on our current malaise have been astute about the material—the conventionally *political*—reasons for the strongman's rise. Fully to understand it and begin to combat it, we need to comprehend something about the emotional hold the strongman exerts on the population. Political analysis revolving around interest groups, budgets, and policies is important, but it is not enough. There are periods in history when emotional factors become as important, maybe more important, than material ones. Ours is one of them. At certain times, analyses based in psychological terms such as regression, fixation, the super-ego, and the id would be of minor import, maybe even beside the point. Alas, this is not that time. Happy are the political and cultural periods to which Freud's analysis is irrelevant.

Some may say that the era of Trump and leaders like him is coming to an end. It was a blip on the screen. But as long as we can do nothing about the crisis of authority that Arendt and Nietzsche describe, the possibility for the return of the bizarre figure who somehow blends super-ego with id is all too strong.

Politics and the Super-Ego 2: Social Justice

The super-ego can be an affliction. It can also be a weapon.

The terms of the affliction are probably obvious by now. When the super-ego is inflamed, the subject becomes the object of endless self-criticism. The unwanted guest takes over the premises and trashes them. There is unceasing pressure on the self to be perfect. Can you act? Often not, because no action could possibly satisfy the demands of the over-I.

The writer sits before his keyboard unmoving: nothing he could write will meet the inner standard that tyrannizes him. He's frozen. He's afflicted with what he calls writer's block, a salient instance of super-ego torment. And there is little he can do. He writes a word, a sentence—and then strikes it out. How foolish, how inadequate. Surely it's unequal to the brilliance that he rightly (rightly!) demands of himself. After hours spent in the overpriced Aeron chair, which is to him an implement of torture, he rises berating himself for failing once again. He's paralyzed, and no force in the world, it seems, can get him unstuck.

He judges himself harshly in all regions and sometimes is proud of it. He was raised by his parents and then educated by his teachers to be attuned to the privileges he possesses as a White male from a prosperous and educated family. A woman, a White woman, can be comparably attuned. All through school, they both learned that the history of their country is a history of oppression—conquest, enslavement, exploitation. And they feel, deeply, how they are implicated in these past crimes. Super-ego judgment rings down on them, and it is of course an inward judgment that they cannot escape. There is no hiding from the super-ego. The subject feels profoundly guilty, tortured, miserable. And as the days go by, it gets worse. The inability to get anything worthy done hurts, too. The locked-down feeling from being prey to personal and social standards that one cannot meet becomes insufferable. The reign of the over-I grows.

What is to be done?

My speculation is this. The individual often resolves—or tries to resolve—the personal crisis of the super-ego by projecting its judgments away from him- or herself, out into the world and onto others. This is manifest in taking extreme political and social positions and trying to enforce them on all within reach. It often consists in being hypersensitive on behalf of the purportedly oppressed—often without consulting them. One is alert to the tiniest infractions. A slightly insensitive joke on TV or online provokes a blizzard of Twitter invective. The misuse of a pronoun—dead naming, it's sometimes called—sends the defender of the oppressed into paroxysms of anger and sorrow. Being sensitive to the most miniscule of infractions allows the world—and the self—to believe that one is comparably attuned to all forms of injustice. Someone who takes fiery exception to a stray remark on an out-of-the-way website must certainly be committed to justice on every level.

And perhaps the subject's grief is authentic. Maybe he is deeply committed to the cause. Such people do exist. But by their works you shall know them. The truly committed are generally out doing practical deeds for others. They support progressive candidates, give their money to promising initiatives, help feed the hungry, help shelter those without roofs of their own. They are active in the world, and their actions come out of compassion, not a need to absolve the ego. They are to be admired.

But many people are slaves to the super-ego. Their engagement with social and political issues is symbolic and not pragmatic. They want to control what can and cannot be said, can and cannot be done. They are more interested in statues, pronouns, and symbols than in the welfare of the poor. They want the power of judges over their fellows. They wish to be super-egos in their own right: walking, talking, blogging, podcasting super-egos. Nietzsche describes such unfortunate beings in *Thus Spake Zarathustra:* "Mistrust all in whom the impulse to punish is powerful. They are people of low sort and stock: the hangman and the bloodhound look out of their faces. Mistrust all who talk much of their justice! Verily, their souls lack more than honey. And when they call themselves the good and the just, do not forget that they would be pharisees, if only they had—power."

By judging, one gets rid of the burden of being self-judged, if only for a while. When you deploy the super-ego in the world, you gain some temporary relief. You judge and you judge, and for a while it seems that your sins have been forgiven. You feel light, walk with a bounce in your step. All is well. Judges are generally not shadowed by guilt, at least when they are judging. Says Nietzsche, "Out of every one of their complaints sounds revenge; in their praise there is always a sting, and to be a judge seems bliss to them."

But here is the problem. Becoming the super-ego seems to strengthen the agency. It's a bit like a muscle: the more it's used the more potent it becomes. And then, when the quiet moments arrive, it turns itself back on the ego with redoubled strength. All of the self-hatred begins again. What seemed an escape route—the attempt to humiliate others as one has been and is humiliated by the over-I—does not work, and the subject is left alone and self-hating.

Super-ego warriors—a more accurate term, I fear, than social justice warriors—can be powerful figures. There is something in all of us that is guilty, self-critical, discontent, and they can readily tap into it.

They form an alliance with what is most self-disliking in other selves. They exert a fascination. The sane (the relatively sane) are often drawn to them as by a bizarre magnetism. Thus one super-ego warrior sometimes makes more in his image, a kind of zombie effect. What's needed isn't castigation of this peculiar tribe, so much as compassion for them, and an explanation of how and why the judging faculty can slip the bounds of sanity. From this, relative freedom might arise.

Politics and the Super-Ego 3:
The Blessed and the Damned

In America now, we have a class of people who have every reason to be unhappy with themselves. Members of the White working class, especially men, are failing by their own standards. The good jobs are gone. The once plentiful union work that made life well worth living all through the country, but especially in what's now called the Rust Belt, has disappeared, displaced by global outsourcing and automation. Poverty has arrived where there used to be plenty. Drug addiction and suicide have become commonplace. Life expectancy for White male Americans without college degrees is dropping—a shocking fact.

Says Anne Case, coauthor of *Deaths of Despair and the Future of Capitalism:* "every year about 150,000 Americans die from suicide, drug overdose, and alcoholic liver disease. . . . There is a lot of pain, rising mental health issues, family lives that have come apart, a loss of community." Case's collaborator Angus Deaton describes the cause in simple terms: "a slow and steady deterioration in job prospects and in wages."

People are hurting materially. They work two jobs and still can't pay the bills; their kids can't find work; families are broken apart; everyone knows somebody who has gone over to addiction. It feels like the world's been kicked in. And yet the old standards remain: one must have a good job, support one's family, drink and do drugs within bounds, help one's neighbor—and above all, never complain.

This is hard to bear. Failing in life by the standard set by oneself and one's family can be killing. I couldn't keep my job. I couldn't keep my marriage together. I lost my kids to social services. My father died of heart disease—he was fifty-three. Such events are intolerable, and they frequently owe more to fate and uncontrollable economic configurations than anything else. No working person could have stopped those jobs from disappearing. As the Bruce Springsteen song goes, "Foreman said these jobs are going boy, and they ain't coming back." That's his hometown, and mine (Malden, Massachusetts), and plenty of others as well.

All of this might be bearable. One might be able to suffer it through, even if one is raging at oneself internally. But another factor makes it nearly unendurable. And that is the contempt of the lucky ones, the prosperous ones, the rich and educated. They see White working people, White poor people, as valueless, soon to die out or be replaced by immigrants who better suit their hopes. In the most polite company, you can say exactly what you like about "rednecks": they are fair game at all times. The people I work with as a university professor are kind, thoughtful, intelligent, and humane. But they have a blind spot for the sufferings of the White working class. They castigate them as racist, sexist, homophobic, and all the rest, without bothering to get to know any of them in person and find out whether this might be true.

The White one-time working-class knows this and feels it in part because their tribunes, the likes of Sean Hannity and Tucker Carlson, never stop telling them so. They hate you. They hold you in contempt. They think you are no better than animals. You think this country is your home, but they want you out of here. You are no more than dirt to them. Or as 45 liked to say, "They despise you." And often they do.

And sometimes, being who they are, suffering what they have suffered, these people are dirt to themselves. To hear an outside voice, an educated one at that, echoing their own self-loathing is unsupportable. How can one bear it? One answer is to take revenge. And revenge means sticking it to the wine-sipping classes by going to the ballot box and voting for the strongman and his allies. You show up at his rallies and cheer maniacally because it hurts the elite so much. And you worship him like a demigod, for many reasons, but in part because it's such a kick in the pants to the brightly shining good ones, who are actually demons of contempt and dismissal. You rebel against your own interior over-I, and also against the cultural over-I that tells you from every direction and in the most refined accents that you are worthless.

My neighbor about a mile down the road has a sign on the back of his pick-up truck that says, "Don't let liberal scum run your life." He's an intelligent guy on some level, a reader, has a degree from a good college, likes to think things through for himself.

Liberals are trying to tell my neighbor what to do on an ethical level. They're trying to boss him around. They have opinions about what he ought to say and what he ought to eat and the vehicle he ought to drive and the way he ought to regard the other gender (or genders). They want him to avoid one set of words and embrace another set. And the words, proscribed and endorsed, seem to change every week. They want to mess with basic bathroom protocols. They want to outlaw jokes. They aspire to get in his head and judge him nonstop.

He would like to evict them, but I'm not sure that he really knows how. Once they're in there, they're in. Liberals want to work their way into the interstices of consciousness, and getting them out can't be easy. My neighbor—we've talked a little about this—is oppressed by the weight of instruction and prohibition that he feels within. What his bumper sticker really means, I think, is that he doesn't want liberals running his life, but they're doing it anyway.

How does one respond? Perhaps you borrow a phrase from Huck Finn and say: "All right then, I'll go to hell." If you think me a demon, I'll be a demon; think me ignorant and stubborn, I'll be more so; think me a fool, I'll be three times a fool. And every day I'll drive you crazy by endorsing the vulgar, vain personage who sat in Lincoln's office and may again. I'll pretend that he's a Christian when I know he's no more so than Pontius Pilate was. I'll pretend he cares about me and mine, when I know that he truly cares only about one human integer on the planet. I'll pretend he makes sense when he doesn't. I'll declare he's a statesman when I know he's a scammer. I'll pretend he won the 2020 election, even though I know better. All this I'll do to get back at the pompous characters who spend their time judging me. Trump is a vulgar super-ego to pit against the Puritan super-ego that operates out of Yale, the *New York Times*, and the Democratic Party.

On some level, I believe that people like my neighbor know they are acting in a sort of play. But maybe it does keep some of the self-hate at a distance. Meanwhile the globe heats up, plagues come on apace, the rich get very rich, the poor do what they are all too well accustomed to doing—suffering and wanting in the midst of plenty. In the war of the obscenely inflamed id against the refined and brutal over-I, who really wins?

Are the Kids Alright?

I love my students—I surely do. But there is no way I would want to be one of them, or a part of what's now being called "Generation Z."

They're stepping into the arena grossly underequipped to fight: no sword, no shield, no strategy. I would arm them better if I could.

When I begin to think about my students, two words come to mind. One is "success." The other is "performance." Their opposites matter, too—but we'll get to that.

From the time they stepped into preschool, the great majority of my students have been primed for success. What does success mean? The answer to that question is rather distressingly simple. Success means getting into a top-tier college. My school, the University of Virginia, isn't among the topmost, but it qualifies. To "get in," one needs to do certain things: generate A's, participate in activities, become a "leader," win the support of the influential adults in one's life.

The As come first. It is important to get as many as possible and to do so in what are ostensibly the most challenging courses. You must excel. But (and here is the important point) you need to excel numerically. You need good grades. That does not mean that you need to learn much. You may learn in calculus and chemistry. Given the rigor of the testing in those subjects, there is probably no other choice. But for other subjects, learning is not necessary. History, English, social sciences—those rely on writing and reading, and here you have multiple options. You can read all the books, you can do your writing yourself. You can learn and grow and develop as a writer and thinker. You can assess your strengths and weaknesses; consult with your teacher; get together with friends to talk, compare notes, and improve your powers.

But if you do that, you take a risk. It takes a lot of time. And without that time, you're in trouble. How do you show up for your activities? How do you make it daily to lacrosse practice? How do you make it to prom committee? Tutoring kids downtown: that takes time, but the admissions office wants to see service. It might also be good to chill out occasionally—and also get online and curate your social media presence, which is critically important in the world of performance and success.

The problem is this: with all the time that it takes to succeed in current terms, there is little left for the actual, arduous, often pleasurable work of learning. Learning takes time, but time is not readily to be had. So one turns to *Spark Notes* and something called *Shmoop* to get an angle on Shakespeare. All of one's difficult reading can get jobbed off in one way or another. If you are reasonably adroit, knowing the plot and the characters is often enough to get you your A. But you do not learn anything. You will succeed, but you will probably not grow, except in developing tactics for success.

It is too early for us to tabulate the result of developing a class of young people who, smart, energetic, and charming as they may be, have not developed a true taste for reading. Reading is valuable in a hundred different ways, but one of those ways is, for the present and near future, salient. When you read well, you get off by yourself and you engage in a dialogue with the writer. You concur, you doubt, you resist. And in that process of solitary reading a major development occurs. You slowly, sometimes without noticing it, begin to assemble a private self, a self that is surely touched by prevailing opinion but is not determined by it. You learn how to say no to the established patterns of belief; or at the very least, you learn how to issue a thoughtful "maybe" and continue to ponder the question. You develop, to borrow a phrase from Lionel Trilling, an "opposing self," at least when opposition is required. You learn to think for yourself—and if the development of informed, self-aware, independent thinkers is not a major objective of humanistic education, then nothing is.

If you do not read, deeply and privately, you risk becoming prey to every attractive social consensus that sputters down the highway. You'll become one of those oversocialized beings who cannot step apart and think something through for yourself. In short, you'll become an easy mark for the super-ego and the forces in society that support and reflect it.

Or you can resist. Thinking of his ideal student, the American Scholar, Emerson writes, "Let him not quit his belief that a popgun is a popgun, though the ancient and honorable of the earth affirm it to be the crack of doom. In silence, in steadiness, in severe abstraction, let him hold by himself; add observation to observation, patient of neglect, patient of reproach; and bide his own time,—happy enough, if he can satisfy himself alone he has seen something truly."

If you take the currently conventional path, you'll be committing yourself to performance. You will need to create and to curate an image—as perfect, poised, and enviable as possible. Adam Phillips says that we no longer know what the good life might be, so instead we try to create an enviable life. We post the pictures that make us look beautiful—like members of the elite, like people with the world all before us, and ours for the keeping. So the creation of the image becomes paramount in the lives of the young: one performs the enviable life. And of course one succeeds in such a way as to feed the idealized, enviable profile.

Students constantly worry about their online profiles. It's not only about keeping them buff, it's also about reacting aptly to events.

When the political wind blows, one must go with it. After the murder of George Floyd, many of my students felt it was necessary to post items in solidarity with the movement. What if one was not in complete solidarity? One must post something, something, something. Keeping silent was not an option. One must respond to the ever-whirling force of social pressure. Students speak with a mix of irony and acquiescence about the need to be "performative." One must look right, tweet right, post right, succeed in the right way.

Thin success (all those A's) and performative triumph are super-ego functions. Lacan tells us what happens when the very young child confronts a mirror image of himself. He loves what he sees: the image in the glass is charming, beautiful, yet also coherent. It hangs together, possesses unity, is one. What a joy to see oneself there. We can all recall the sight of an early toddler recognizing himself in the mirror. He points and laughs and throws back his heavy head and laughs some more. For the image is wonderful.

Yet the image does not represent the child's internal experience. Internally the baby is full of turbulence—he needs, wants, feels pain, feels strange pleasure, is achingly confused, is wild with delight. So are we all, one might say. Though for the child new to his body and new to the world, the experience of turbulent inner life is no doubt especially intense. The mirror, with its calm, liquid surface, solves all those problems, in a way. The child loves the perfection of the image but also feels the disjunction between the tumult he experiences within and the composure he sees in the glass.

Lacan indicates that the child will strive all his life to regain that superficial image of perfection. He will try to create an outer image of himself that is as appealing to himself and others as the personage he sees in the glass. He will attempt to succeed in superficial ways; he'll perform so that others will look at him and nod approval. He will look to that super-ego-responsive image and do all he can to make it his, and the world's, insofar as the world is looking—and one almost always feels that it is. He will perform. He will succeed.

The other route, the difficult route, he will be inclined to abjure: this is not the route of succeeding and performing, but the route of authenticity. Learning is hard—and it begins with a perception of the self that does not sit well with self-love. To learn, we have to accept that we are ignorant. There is much we do not know. We are partial, incomplete. It's even possible that much of what we claim to know is not so. We have been duped before, and we no doubt can be again. And it is not always the mountebank with his pack of cards or the tout with his tips that leads us down the path. It is often ourselves.

To actually learn, rather than merely succeed at something that resembles learning, we need to admit that the dazzling image in the mirror of our psyches is a lure and a deception. We need to be willing to accept that what is inside—turbulence, doubt, and even some rank confusion—comes much closer to defining us than any ready-to-hand self-idealization. Learners are by definition imperfect. They have a long way to go. And also there is this: at a certain point in learning, one begins to know that one will never reach perfection's promised land. Lillian Hellman called herself an "unfinished woman." It is a blessing to the self—and a hard one—to think of ourselves as always and forever unfinished. We'll never coincide with the glowing, super-ego–approved image in our mind.

The super-ego is emphatic: we must always be perfect. If we offer it counterfeit perfection—success, performance—perhaps it half-smiles. The ideal of perfection stands against the idea of a human being as an incomplete being, an open project, that throws itself into life to see what might be done. This indeterminate self is, one might imagine, what the super-ego abjures. Also, we might speculate, the super-ego detests authenticity, which is in many ways the dialectical opposite of performance. The authentic individual has it as a matter of faith to stay true to her perceptions. If she sees it, and she considers it, and she submits it to the best critique available, then it is up to her to stick with it. To be authentic means to love truth. It is to pursue truth with ardor, with the conviction that it can be found. And when you find it, try not to back down. Authenticity, learning: in their commitment to fragment and partiality, they challenge the hegemony of super-ego perfection.

Simone de Beauvoir and Jean-Paul Sartre, inspirations perhaps to Lacan, launch their critique at what we might call self-objectification. There is something in us that wants to freeze rather than flow. We want to be a thing, a being that does not change, that exists in perfect form the way natural objects do, "rocks and stones and trees," as the poet says. It's tempting to make of oneself an object: one can escape the pressure of mortality—for an object never changes, never decays, never dies. It never leaves the world. It is what Queen Elizabeth I wished to be: *semper eadem*, always the same.

Against the lure of being-in-itself, one pits the arduous exertions of being-for-itself. Being-for-itself chooses its goals, picks its project, and throws itself into life, however apparently absurd or prone to failure the project may be. However absurd, it is mine and I am ready to define myself by it and be defined by it. The project is open-ended and personal, and has a very good chance of failing. In fact, choosing a project that ultimately will not end up in a measure of failure may be a weakness of character, One wants to be the nation's great scholar, or athlete, or composer—and into the effort she throws all that she can muster. For what truly fascinates us, focuses our energies, and confers meaning is a highly difficult goal that is nonetheless not impossible to reach. And to go further, maybe the prospect of honorable failure can fascinate too. If only, if only, I could pull this off.

For my students, for the young, to move from the shadow of the super-ego would be to move from success and performance to learning and authenticity. Is such a move possible in the super-ego–riddled culture in which we find ourselves? These are questions for the final section of the book.

For now, we might say that to know what's wanted—an end to mirror games, the beginning of something else—perhaps gets us a step down the road.

Identity!

For my students, performance and success are the major super-ego aspirations: there is also identity.

Students now are transfixed by *identity*. They want to know who they are, and they spend plenty of their college time trying to figure it out. Am I gay or straight? Or am I some complexly shifting mix of sexual identities? Am I male or female, or perhaps something in between? Maybe I should contemplate changing my gender identity through dress and appearance, or even surgery. Perhaps I'm queer. (But what does being queer mean now, and to me?) Not all of my students have read Judith Butler, but they are all familiar with the view that gender is a matter of performance. If we can perform gender as we like, largely undetermined by hormones and genes, then we presumably can achieve an ultimate freedom of identity.

Perhaps the most salient category for arriving at one's contemporary identity is race. My students are highly conscious of racial terms. Am I Black? Or mixed race? (Most African Americans could claim either of these identities.) If I have a sixteenth Cherokee blood, is it legitimate to call myself Native American? Can I say I'm a member of the tribe when there may be tribe members who don't think that one-sixteenth is enough?

What my students' identity quests have in common is that the terms of demarcation tend to be group terms. One affiliates with one or more groups, and in so doing finds oneself, finds an *identity*.

After a graduation not long ago, I ran into a student I'm particularly fond of. She was wearing a red stole from the Asian Pacific American Students' Association, a purple cord to signify affiliation with the LGBTQ+ community, and an orange stole for graduating in three years or fewer. African-American students wear a kente cloth; there's a cord for the athletic honor roll, one for the academically elite Echols Scholars, and various other designations. Groups and groups: twenty years ago at graduation, one might have glimpsed a Phi Beta Kappa key, but that would have been about it.

Some find the results of young people's current quests for identity through group affiliation to be slightly comic. In her illuminating book *Kill All Normies: Online Culture Wars from 4Chan and Tumblr to Trump and the Alt-Right*, Angela Nagle discusses some of the more striking gender identities that have emerged from Tumblr blog posts. They include Alexigender, gender identity that is fluid between more than one gender, but the individual cannot tell what those genders are; Ambigender, a feeling of two genders simultaneously, but without fluidity; and Anxiegender, a gender affected by anxiety. And we're still in the A's.

Nagle provides a remarkably good-humored guide to online cultures, but even she smiles at some of the gender categories she encounters. I smile too. But I'm with Henry David Thoreau when he says, "I desire that there be as many different persons in the world as possible; but I would have each one be very careful to find out and pursue *his own way,* and not his father's, or his mother's, or his neighbor's instead."

As a teacher, I applaud my students' quest for identity. The quest often provokes tough-minded introspection, plenty of conversation online and off-, and sometimes brave declarations that parents and friends are surprised or even shocked by. My students' terms for discovering and disclosing identity are not my terms, or my generation's. How could they be? I can only step back and cheer when, after long introspection, a young person makes a declaration of identity.

But identity is not enough. To put the matter crudely, once one decides who one is, one must decide what one will do. A discovery or disclosure of identity can be a brilliant first step, and it matters for many reasons. But it matters chiefly because locating one's identity clears the decks, establishes some measure of inner peace, and puts one in a position to do one's work in the world. "But do your thing," says Emerson, "and I shall know you."

The quest to find and consolidate an identity, and then leave it at that, is a super-ego–driven quest. It's an attempt to delimit the ego—freeze it and put it in a box. The terms for most identity quests are group terms—and super-ego values inhere in group formations. To consolidate self and go no further is a surrender to conformity and regimented virtue.

The hunger to consolidate one's sense of self is a hunger that Freud would both understand and question. The very word *identity* indicates a problem, suggesting as it does a coherence and stability of self. Identity connotes unity, consistency, a fullness and presence of being that can abide through time. Freudian thinking finds the concept of unity within the self untenable and potentially destructive.

To Freud, we are not and can never be one: we are at least three persons. Character is conflict among the three agencies of the self—and the conflict is ongoing. To recap a bit, Freud describes human beings as composed of super-ego, ego, and id. To put it crudely, the ego desires stability, the id makes the claims of appetite, and the super-ego, as we have seen, judges all, including judging the often sane judge that is the ego. Each of these three beings has a different relation to consciousness. Freud wants to tell us that super-ego and id are largely unconscious, but by the middle of his career he is also talking about the unconscious dimension of the ego. The three agencies contend with each other, often beyond the realm of our awareness. Add to this inner strife the turbulence that tends to arise when horrible, traumatic memories suddenly emerge and disrupt what equanimity we might have.

We are not stable. We are not still. We are churning, fluctuating creatures. Can we actually know ourselves? Yes, but often in fits and starts. Intelligence matters, as do experience and learning. But the idea that through insight or psychotherapy or Buddhist meditation or significant doses of opiates we can ever still the inner self—Freud finds that notion absurd.

The notion of identity, now so popular among those who look for it in gender and race and sexuality, implies the possibility of resolving the self in some binding manner. If Freud is right and the psyche is always churning, then it can never be fixed in such a way that one can claim an identity. We are simply too changeful for that: the civil war within the psyche goes on and on.

But what is the harm of claiming identity? From Freud's point of view, it is a form of hubris. It suggests a self-resolution that humans cannot achieve. A person who believes that he's achieved identity is likely to be overbearingly confident. She knows who she is. She's got herself all figured out. And from such feelings of coherence and correctness are likely to come assertions, exclamations, dictates. It is not surprising that the advocates of identity are often such aggressively confident dispensers of their views. How could they be wrong? They know precisely who and what they are. And knowing that, they must know more besides. They are awake. Others live in a dream, waiting to be rescued by loudly administered doses of the real.

Freud does not care for our hubris: to him the human self is an enigma. We cannot solve it, but we can move toward better comprehension. What we do not know about our conflicted, unconscious selves ought to make us both curious and humble. Not that we should deny our every perception; but we should surely doubt our assertions, especially as they tend to the dogmatically universal. Freud may be the best antidote we have to the current forms of political hubris.

Super-Ego Drugs: Adderall and Amphetamines

I had spring and fall allergies for some time, bad ones. My head filled up, my nose ran, I sneezed and coughed and sneeze-coughed. The worst part was what happened to my eyes: they started to itch early in the morning and kept it up all day. I went at them until my sockets were red and aching. My head felt like it was on fire, I couldn't breathe half well enough.

I hate taking over-the-counter drugstore meds. But for these allergies, which have since gone the way of the West Wind, there was no other choice. I took a red droplet of a pill that was called Sudafed. It beat back the allergic symptoms well enough that I could go about my modest business. The drug also made me disposed to pay my bills. Honestly. Pay my bills.

Under the influence of the little red helper I could merrily go to my office, sit down, and rip off twenty or so checks—these being the days when all payment went through the mail. I won't say I loved paying the bills on little red, but it gave me satisfaction. I felt efficient, useful, tuned in, slightly righteous. When the allergies receded in the winter, I would still pop a red on bill day. I wrote those checks fast and accurately, and when it was all over I patted myself affectionately on the back—or something did.

That was not quite me, the person who paid those bills with such dash. Money issues sometimes send me spinning and even now I don't much relish relinquishing cash, even for the best of causes—

groceries, mortgage, tuition. But I was treed no longer. Under the tutelage of little red, I was a dutiful clerk, not the Bartleby, I-would-prefer-not-to type I had been before and would go back to being as soon as my liver washed red out of my bloodstream.

Little red, it turns out, went on to become a crucial ingredient in methamphetamine, a drug that makes you feel like you've been shot from a cannon. As I learned in time, little red went quite a way to approximate the effects of amphetamine-style drugs like Adderall, which millions now take for what's called ADD, attention deficit disorder.

I found that when I was under the influence of Sudafed (can you be said to be "under the influence" of an over-the-counter allergy drug?), it was not hard to do the things my super-ego wanted me to do. I could pay the bills, but I was also happy to clean the bathroom; launder, dry, fold, and store my clothes; and run (sometimes truly *run*) all sorts of errands. I took considerable and rather pathetic satisfaction in performing these tasks.

I had turned myself into a minion of my super-ego and was acting in a way that made it happy—or so I infer. The super-ego does not function without opposition. We feel its presence in day-to-day life and sense its demands. But often we rebel. We simply don't wanna! Apparently, not only does the super-ego oppress the ego, the ego tries to fight back, by being a stubborn child and resisting the whims of the patriarchal, matriarchal, anarchical squalling over-I. Little red got my psyche into temporary alignment, at least from the over-I's point of view. I became a temporary serf to the super-ego.

And maybe that holds a clue to all the ADD diagnoses and all the Adderall prescriptions now prolific in the world. The ego says I don't wanna, and the over-I says you must, and there is, it turns out, a solution. Take one of these—they're time-release—and if you need another, by all means take two. The super-ego will assume command, rather gently all things considered, the ego will recede, but only a bit, and you'll be happy, happy, happy. And more productive, too.

Now if you'd like an id drug . . . well, that's another story.

Is it any great surprise that these super-ego drugs are so widespread? The over-I got too strong and asks too much of us—and the ego rebels. Sometimes the only way to answer the call is with some assistance—the inner drillmaster's assistant. Father's Little Helper.

What those hits of Sudafed enabled me to do was quite simple: they enabled me to *pay attention*. And in the culture of the super-ego, attention is at a premium.

How much about our situation within a super-ego culture may be locked in the simple, commonplace instruction "Pay attention"? To have been a student is to have heard the phrase directed at you. To be a parent or teacher (or doctor, lawyer, judge, cop, priest, minister, or imam) is inevitably to have uttered the abrupt, hortatory line: Pay attention!

Is "Pay attention!" more common now than it was a decade or two ago? One wouldn't be surprised if it is. "Attention" has become a critical term at the center of a multitude of social issues and human concerns. We are disposed to worry about the fragmented minds of the young. We wonder if texting-while-viewing-while-talking-while-eating and never being just one place at any time may be having a deleterious effect on the young. Are they incapable of concerted focus? Are they unable to sit and think? Have they been driven (by distraction) to distraction?

Pay attention! The phrase bears some considering. In the essay "On Truth and Lies in a More than Moral Sense," Nietzsche makes an acute observation on the way language works. Language, he tells us, is a mobile host of metaphors and metonyms that have become conventional over time. Words become like coins that have been worn plain from overuse. We no longer see the tropes embedded in our language.

Here is one such trope: attention is something that must be paid. Paying attention is similar to discharging a debt, offering tribute, or giving the entity that demands the attention something akin to cash. When you tell someone to pay attention you are trying to take something from her, something that, one might assume, she does not wish to give: her focus, her presence of mind, her full being. Is it possible that paying attention is akin to paying tribute? When someone asks you to pay attention, they are imposing authority on you. Perhaps it is not that we can't get ourselves to focus on this matter or that, but simply that offering attention is felt as a challenge, a burden. "I made myself pay attention, even though what he was saying was boring." "It wasn't easy to pay attention to him, but I did." There's a tribute involved. There's a tax, a debt. Do you understand? Are you paying attention to me? We can take satisfaction in paying a bill or getting rid of a debt, but while it may be a relief, it is never exactly a joy.

Is it surprising, then, that people have difficulties conferring attention? Attention is a discipline, a compulsion, and of course a bodily posture. One stands at attention. The drill sergeant shrieks, the cadet hops to and makes his body into a pillar. He's now a missile, a pole, a strong and well-disciplined I. Standing at attention hurts (at least after a while), though it no doubt has its satisfactions, too. The super-ego exerts control over the body, and the body obeys.

Many feel that the discipline of attention—and common usage shows us that it is a discipline—is in short supply. We bemoan the fact that young people (and sometimes we ourselves) cannot sit down and focus. We blame it on the Internet and social media and a permissive culture geared too much to pleasure and too little to discipline. We say that we're sick. Our culture has attention deficit disorder.

What's the opposite of attention? What are we doing when we cannot pay attention? We are distracted, of course. The opposite of attention is distraction. When we ought to be homing in on one thing, our mind is romping through many. (Samuel Taylor Coleridge complimented William Wordsworth for being "all man" and for his ability to "do one thing at a time.") Maybe. Maybe distraction is the scattered, regrettable reverse side of attention, but I'm not quite sure that resolves matters.

I'd say rather that the deep opposite of attention isn't distraction, but absorption. No one ever tells you to "pay absorption." Absorption is what occurs when you immerse yourself in something you love. The artist and the poet and the philosopher and the scientist become absorbed. The kind doctor becomes absorbed in her patient; the teacher is absorbed in his class presentation. The musician becomes absorbed in the fugue. When that happens, time stops and one lives in an ongoing present. One feels whole and at one with oneself. The little boy drawing with his pad on the floor, tongue out from one side of his mouth, is a picture of absorption. He is not really paying attention. He is absorbed. What is happiness? The poet W. H. Auden answered this quite simply: Happiness comes in absorption.

Happiness is losing yourself in something you love and that will also in all probability come to benefit others. Happiness is working in an honorable vocation. Happiness is helping others, protecting others, or enhancing the stock of humane knowledge. Happiness is absorption.

When you're involved in absorbing tasks, you do sometimes have to "pay attention." You've got to proofread the novel; you've got to check and recheck your patient's chart; you've got to clean your French horn and tune your guitar. The capacity to pay attention is critical to the life of absorption. Bertrand Russell thought it rather brutal to teach children how to sit and focus, but he understood that in later life, so much good could come from the capacity to make yourself present and quiet that he was willing to recommend that all teachers teach the arts of getting your legs under the desk and your hands on top.

"Teach us," T. S. Eliot says, "to sit still."

But Russell thought that learning to pay attention was a form of dues: a cost one pays for access to the best that life offers, the capacity to be absorbed.

If you ask people only to pay attention—that is, to obey their super-egos all the time—they will almost inevitably resist. Attention is an imprisoning of the mind. If you don't put attention to a higher purpose—one associated with absorption—the mind will rebel and so will the heart. In our culture I believe we ask too many people to pay attention too much of the time—and give them back nothing but a salary. If you have to sit at a computer from one end of the day to the other, doing tasks that bore you, you are likely to have a hard time paying attention. Your mind will wander; your fantasies roam. Humans cannot live exclusively on the bread and water of attention. The student is sent to the computer, where she must complete one boring task after another with her mind locked into a tiny rectangular space. Her attention will grow deficient, unless you juice her with drugs that lock her inside the mental prison. Later she will take a job that strongly resembles her schooling: all attention, no absorption. Her mind will wander. Her boss and her teachers and maybe even her spouse will tell you that she has a *deficit.* It's interesting how the idiom of cash leaks into our talk about mental focus. One "pays" attention. One possesses an attention "deficit." (Susan Sontag liked to say that she had "attention surplus disorder.") Then there is talk about cultural crisis and failures of education.

But those discussions miss the point. Our compulsively productive culture of the super-ego leaves fewer and fewer opportunities for absorption. Under the reign of the computer in its super-ego guise, jobs are more and more about attention: get it right, focus on the details, fill out the chart and revise it. If attention does not lead to absorption, or if there is little possibility for absorption in a given life, then there will be deficits of attention.

I'm neither a medical doctor nor a psychologist, and I cannot comment with any authority on the discovery or prevalence of the condition called attention deficit hyperactivity disorder. It may be biologically based. It may result from the stresses of a difficult childhood. The best discussion of its possible causes that I have read is by the Canadian physician Gabor Mate, and he leaves the question open.

But I will say this. If ADHD is to some degree a biological disorder, there may be social conditions that stimulate and exacerbate it. When young children are denied the physical release of recess and unstructured play, when they are burdened prematurely with homework and excessive cognitive labor, are we not creating conditions in which healthy children are bound to appear—if not become—distracted, inattentive, and even hyperactive? When our super-ego culture asks people to do grinding, meaningless work of the mind, often within the tiny confines of a computer screen, it is not surprising if their minds rebel. When you compel people to cut cane or plant cotton under a broiling sun, their bodies eventually rebel and begin to fail. The mind is like a muscle. The wrong kind of pursuits maintained for too long will exhaust it. Exhausted, the body will function at half capacity: it will sputter and churn. Doesn't the mind's churning inattention that ADHD brings remind one of the body's clumsiness when it's weary?

In *The Human Condition*, Hannah Arendt makes a distinction between work and labor. Work is dignified and self-recreating; labor is demeaning and breaks the self down. There is work of the mind. There is labor of the mind too.

But, some might counter, there is absorption in our culture. And plenty of it. Only look at the face of the young man watching TV, the young girl at the movies, the kid in his basement playing a first-person shooter video game. Isn't this absorption?

I think not. It is important to distinguish between being absorbed and being mesmerized. One can be mesmerized, enchanted, visually inebriated: the condition is not hard to bring on. In a super-ego culture that asks us too often to "pay attention," we can find rest and release through electronic diversion. Paying attention should ideally be rewarded by absorption, but when absorption isn't available, or no one teaches us how to achieve it, being mesmerized will have to do. Being mesmerized is all about wish-fulfillment. It's about becoming the soldier, the knight, the sports star, the princess. It is a turning away from reality. To be absorbed is to intensify one's connection with what is real, in the hope of reshaping it for the better. The engaged and absorbed doctor wants health for his patient; the scientist wants to add to the stock of available knowledge; the poet hopes to bring beauty and truth, pleasure and instruction, to her readers. These people are not cheering themselves up or inflating their sense of self. They are acting out of love for the world, and in return they are receiving one of life's best gifts, simple absorption. And they are also, if only briefly, suspending the culture of the super-ego.

Internet!

How did the Internet become a super-ego machine? It could have gone many other ways.

Maybe it's best to begin by thinking of the Internet, borrowing a term from Marshall McLuhan, as potentially a global village. In a global village we are committed to exchange. We swap wisdom and information; we exchange goods and services; we exchange warm wishes and good will. Today we all, or almost all, live in the same village. We are part of a tribe. We are, in a manner of speaking, One.

If you know how to use the Internet, you can draw a great deal from the global village. It teems with information, some of it accurate. You can explore, learn, develop in a dozen different directions. And this is all to the good.

News travels quickly on the Internet. Some of it is true—and if you know how to look, maybe most of what you encounter will be true. The technology is an astonishing resource. McLuhan teaches that media are extensions of the human. The shovel extends the arm and hand; the steam shovel provides a superextension of hand and arm. Not for nothing do we call a revolver a firearm.

And the Internet, what would McLuhan say about that? He'd tell us, I suppose, that the Internet is an extension of the human mind. It remembers what we have forgotten—or brings us what we never knew. It calculates numbers beyond our meager capacities. It translates texts from languages we half know or don't know at all. It can make projections into the future that far exceed our scope. It knows so much more than we do—though it is up to us to determine whether what it knows is actually so, and then what to do with that information.

Can the Internet have a psychology? Does it possess an interior life? If the answer is yes, it could only be the one we collectively give it. Perhaps we transfer some part of our psychological life into our electronic technology.

And what kind of life is that? The life of the Internet could easily be defined by openness, creativity, art-making of all kinds. It could be a collaborative work, a festival, a joy. It could be the place where people test their ideas, make their inventions and projections known, to be discussed, developed, adapted. Instead it is often a sink of the most repressive, judgmental bile conceivable. The Internet has become not only a second brain but a second psyche, where judgment, often toxic judgment, reigns.

The Twitter mob in too many ways defines the current Internet. The objective of the mob is to stamp out apostasy. We are righteous. We are correct. We conform to the current patterns of behavior—and you'd better too. Ultimately, what the mob enforces is manners. One must always say the right thing. Saying the wrong thing will be punished, often through official channels. The objective of the Twitter mob is not merely to vilify but to ruin the career and public life of the transgressor. Revealing his crimes to the world matters, but what matters more is connecting with his employer, or possible employers, and destroying his prospects in the world.

The Twitter mob assumes that there is an alliance in place between itself and human resource departments, deans' offices, department chairs, and district supervisors. The idea is to mobilize mob power to conjoin with institutional power. The great triumph is not merely to humiliate this miscreant or that in public. The great triumph is to get him fired. And the more exalted (or "privileged") his position, the better.

There is no embarrassment about ratting to the authorities. The assumption of the Twitter mob is that if they can alert the abiding super-ego–aligned institutions, those institutions will respond sympathetically and do in the transgressor. Let's write to his dean! Let's tell her boss! I'm sure the president of his university would be very interested to hear what he's done. Let's join forces with the day-to-day institutional authorities and get our work done together—or, if they don't do what we demand, turn our fury on them.

There is no attempt at dialogue. The super-ego does not engage in dialogue or seek understanding. Punishment and intimidation is the name of the game. For every poor soul who is pilloried by the mob and then ruined by the authorities, there are hundreds, maybe thousands who melt into silence. The super-ego enjoys punishment; it seems to enjoy turning the subject silent nearly as much, for silence, to the person searching for freedom or truth, is a form of death.

Remember the super-ego as Adam Phillips depicts it, the unwelcome guest at the party. He is judgmental, of course, and literalminded. He does not like complexity or ambiguity. Jokes are his undoing—he does not understand them. He has no idea how to laugh except in sadistic derision. He is, remember Žižek, a figure of obscene enjoyment who pretends to uphold righteous law but is really in the game for the sadistic thrill.

Does anyone stand up to the Twitter mob? Does anyone stand up to the Internet super-ego? Sometimes the victim will make a few self-exculpatory noises, but they are useless. Sometimes he will amuse the mob by apologizing. Mostly he keeps silent and hopes the storm will pass. But in his secret heart of hearts, what he waits for is someone, and maybe a few someones, to step up and defend him. Almost inevitably he waits in vain. Spike Lee, a fine film maker, showed a dram of

humanity and stood up for Woody Allen, a major villain of the Twitter mob. Lee said, in essence, that canceling a great film maker for
crimes that are unproven was a major wrong. I was amazed. Someone
showed courage on the Internet. I wasn't surprised that Spike Lee was
the one to do it. He's been a bold creator all through his career. But in
a few hours everything changed: he was up and online apologizing to
the mob. "My words were WRONG," said the intrepid director. "I do
not and will not tolerate sexual harassment, assault or violence. Such
treatment causes real damage that can't be minimized." No court has
ever found Woody guilty of "sexual harassment, assault or violence,"
but no matter. An often brave, opulently talented, and ferociously
hard-working guy gave in to the mob.

In *Huckleberry Finn*, Mark Twain, speaking through Huck, tells
the story of a lynch mob that goes out after a man named Sherburn.
Sherburn meets them as they come to the front of his house and calls
them what they are: a pack of cowards and fools. He looks them all in
the eye and delivers his verdict on them, and they run like mice.
Twain loved democracy but hated mobs to the bottom of his heart,
and he understood that when you convey power to the people at
large, the mob is always a danger. But he also thought there would be
people who would have the "sand" (Huck's word for courage) to stand
up to them. Look them in the eye and they run—at least sometimes.
But there is no looking the Internet antagonists in the eye. They are
invisible and remote, and always at the ready.

Raymond Chandler once said that whenever a mob went after a
lone individual, he could not help but be on the side of that person no
matter what he might or might not have done. One understands his
point, and for a long time it was a view that many Americans shared.
Hey, back off. Let's have fair play here. Give the guy a chance—let
him tell his side. I fear that this aspect of our national character is in
decline. Instead we have the super-ego–driven mob.

Harper's magazine recently published a collectively signed letter supporting free speech and denouncing the mob. It was a mild document, arguing simply that no one should lose his or her job for maintaining the wrong views. It was hard to disagree with. But the mob was angry. One mob member said that a couple of signatories were hypocritical: they had practiced some of the crimes they decried. They were named. Now, one mob member asked, please let us get together and find as many instances of such hypocrisy as we can about the signers. Send them to me. I'll compile and order and publish.

The enemies of the letter would have looked too shabby simply denouncing its content straight out. And they were not eager to offer direct arguments against it. Doing so would have made them sound like enemies of free speech. So they did all they could to malign the characters of the signers and the character of the publication where the letter appeared. In short order, some of the signatories of the letter defected, genuflecting and asking mercy—but not as many as one might expect: the mob doesn't win every round. But like the over-I, the mob never sleeps and is always ready to jump. They will keep returning until we manage to understand the toxic culture of judgment we've created and do something about it.

I often think of Justine Sacco, who, before boarding a flight from New York to South Africa, tweeted something about how though AIDS was rampant there she wouldn't get it because she was White. The tweet was a joke. She was poking fun at White feelings of invulnerability, mocking what some people call "White privilege." Her tweet was much retweeted until some significant fraction of the Internet had identified her as a racist monster. I suspect that some of her detractors knew she was joking, but they pretended not to. She had no contact with this nastiness while she was in the air, but some zealots elected to go to the airport and meet here there, so as to record, in photographs and texts, the shock she'd experience.

The woman lost her job. She lost her life as previously built. She lost her dignity and perhaps saw the shores of madness. The ringleader of the movement against her claimed he was doing the right thing: if one person's dignity, livelihood, and reputation had to be sacrificed to the cause of antiracism, then so be it. Not much later, the ringleader tweeted something too provocative for current tastes and suffered the same process as Sacco. In this ocean, the fish eat one another and are eaten in their turn.

It's not surprising that we are so prone to judgment—even discounting the force of the strong cultural super-ego.

The world has grown radically complex—perhaps, for some of us, unbearably so. At least it has taken on the *appearance* of boiling complexity. Information comes our way at unprecedented speed and in unprecedented amounts. Step into the world of the Internet and you can see how much blooming, buzzing, laughing, teeth-gnashing, mind-spinning confusion is on offer.

Isn't it natural that we would revert to simplicities and reductions in the face of all this?

The more affairs threaten to run out of control, the more it may help to have not only a firm position but a judgmental temperament. Judgment brings order. We go thumbs-up or thumbs-down and so appear to be the emperors of our own lives. Judgment is a great bulwark against chaos, or the perception of chaos. When we judge profusely and emphatically, we can feel that the world is our domain. Simplification and judgment: these are the ways we hold complexity at bay. Add to this the problem of a ravening cultural super-ego and you have a complex situation.

No one wants to fight the Internet's collective super-ego. If you stand up for a victim, you too will be swept up in the denunciations. Your past utterances and acts will be excavated from corner to corner, and you will find yourself disgraced, with possible loss of your livelihood. And for what? The one who has been charged will get what's coming anyway, and you'll only add another casualty to the war. Besides, you probably do not approve of what the scapegoat said, or at least don't fully concur with it. So why bother? Why go out and play in cybertraffic, where you can be hit and sent spinning?

The best strategy is to push deep into the bunker, wait for the period of shaming to pass, then stick a helmeted head out inch by inch. You consider the odds and hope, probably with reason, that the storm will not settle on you. Then you will be what everyone most wants to be nowadays: safe, if only for a while.

It's possible that all societies have scapegoating rituals. They load a particular weight of perceived sins onto this or that individual, this or that group, and use them to vent their rage. The Internet did not invent the practice. But in our current culture, one sometimes feels that any medium that can be made hospitable to the forces of accusation, judgment, and punishment will be. There is nothing inherently super-ego–disposed about the Internet. We are the ones so disposed, and we fill the medium with our sorrowful, wounded spirits.

The Internet is not only a home for the chaotic, cruel super-ego. It is also the home for rebellion against it. Do the authorities claim that a candidate we don't like has won the election? That couldn't be. It must be corrupt. The count must be wrong. The civil powers are surely in league against the people. The Internet breeds not only the social tyranny of so-called progressives but also the mad response of reactionary minds.

The Internet is, in a sense, at the center of our enquiry into the super-ego. It is where the virtue mob forms; it's where the reactionary spasms against authority take place. It was the 45th president's preferred medium for his unique style of contact with the nation. It's also deeply implicated in the processes that we associate with Foucault's version of the super-ego, social discipline. It's through reference to

Internet-borne models that normative versions of life develop. With the Internet, authorities can gather information about an individual—in the office, the school, the prison, the halfway house—so as to dispense and enforce discipline. It's easier to compel normative identities. The Internet is the place where my students—and many others as well—perform success and display their achievements. It's the source of their standards for what is desirable and what is not. It lets them know how physical perfection looks. It is, in short, the great enforcer of super-ego socialization.

The Super-Ego and the Sense of Time

Do some people lack super-egos? I'm not sure. (Though later we will explore the idea of super-ego transformation.) But there do seem to be literary characters who exist without inner persecution. Shakespeare's Falstaff is one, at least according to W. H. Auden. We first encounter Falstaff awakening in a tavern where he's passed out from drinking. He asks what time it is, and his friend and nemesis, Prince Hal, answers that Falstaff has no business asking the time of day, for the time of day is of no consequence whatever to him. He lives for bawds and capons and wenches, and is as happy to receive them at midnight as he is at midmorning. The marvelous lines go like this:

FALSTAFF: Now, Hal, what time of day is it lad?
PRINCE: Thou art so fat-witted with drinking of old sack, and unbuttoning thee after supper, and sleeping on benches after noon, that thou has forgotten to demand that truly which thou wouldst truly know. What a devil has thou to do with the time of day? Unless hours were cups of sack and minutes capons, and clocks the tongues of bawds, and dials the signs of leaping-houses, and the blessed sun himself a fair hot wench in flame-color'd taffeta; I see no reason why thou shouldst be so superfluous to demand the time of the day.

"What a devil has thou to do with the time of day?" The answer is nothing, or not very much.

Falstaff lives outside the sense of time that makes us dutiful, responsible, committed to the everyday slog. He will have none of it: he has replaced conventional time with drinking, eating, carousing, whoring, and the perpetual exercise of wit. He is, he says, "witty in myself and the cause that wit is in other men." His life is a stream of pleasures, not a sequence of obligations. He lives outside the realm of old ghostly Time, with his hourglass and scythe. As the great Shakespeare critic A. C. Bradley puts it: "The bliss of freedom gained in humour is the essence of Falstaff. His humour is not directed only or chiefly against obvious absurdities; he is the enemy of everything that would interfere with his ease, and therefore of anything serious, and especially of everything respectable and moral. For these things impose limits and obligations, and make us the subjects of old father antic the law, and the categorical imperative, and our station and its duties, and conscience and reputation and other people's opinions, and all sorts of nuisances." Falstaff reduces all imposed obligations to absurdity, and walks about "free and rejoicing." He is the image of an individual who has transcended his super-ego.

Today if we seek for figures who ostensibly have no super-egos, we might find them among celebrities. Celebrities, especially movie stars, pop icons, models, and the like, come to us ageless, untroubled, and radically self-accepting. They are paragons of contented being, not slaves to obsessive doing. We love them for the illusion of freedom they possess but also envy their ostensible autonomy. We are invested in their radiant beings, completely present and unoppressed, but we also savor their falls from grace back into the world of judgment and condemnation.

Shakespeare grasps a crucial fact about the super-ego: it is married to a particular version of time. This is not the time of the seasons or of passing years, or the time spent waiting for a spiritual deliverance of one sort or another. The super-ego is aligned with clock time and all of the commitments and obligations clock time represents. Clock time is about being "on time." It's about being where you are supposed to be at a given hour and minute and then doing what you are supposed to do, effectively, as the boss would like. The super-ego, Freud tells us, is the center of our modern temporal sense.

Do you usually know what time it is without the aid of a timepiece? "Does anybody really know what time it is?" the pop band Chicago asks. "Does anybody really care?" For the space of the song, maybe you don't. Certain experiences can deliver us from constantly knowing what time on the clock it is. Sports, drugs, entertainment, prayer, sex: all can deliver us from the time sense and make it so, in passing, we don't know what time it is and don't much care. These, according to Frank Kermode in *The Sense of an Ending*, are experiences of *Kairos,* redeemed, calm, unanxious time.

But the old god Chronos reasserts himself. He lives outside, in the culture where the temporal demands on us are clear and constant: success is all about showing up, we say—and doing so, we might add, on time. You can assess the strength of your super-ego, I suspect, simply by asking yourself a few times in a day what time it is and then checking. If you are super-ego–ridden, you will be right an appalling number of times.

We want to be "on time." What precisely does that mean? To be on time, I suppose, is to dominate time. We're on it. We have it right. Clichés can be illuminating for the truth they encode, but they convey deceptions too. Someone who is obsessively "on time" is also dominated by time. Time is on him and in him. How can it be that the temporal faculty can become an element of the spirit's identity? Yet it is a part of us. From the day we learn to "tell time" (another fruitful phrase), we come closer to being inhabited by the conventional dynamic of temporality. We are it, it is us. To be on time is one thing. To be obsessed with being on time is surely another.

Similarly, we speak of "having time," as though time were a material possession. We talk about wasting time, as though it were a resource under our control. We talk about time in all sorts of presuming ways. But almost always, in the reign of the super-ego, we talk about time in ways that constitute it as a quantity. We materialize time. We see it as uniform, consistent, something that can be possessed.

Another sort of time that may be under the control of the super-ego is the time between now and one's death. It is possible, maybe inevitable, to be preoccupied with such time. How much do I have left? Will I live another year? Five? Three decades or more? Fears about the life span, about the end, may be associated with the force within that does all it can to make us worried and small—for our protection, of course. What else could it be? Hypochondria, fears of the end, worry, anxiety—all of these may be the legacy of the agency that has been installed in us without our consent. Is it possible to root it out and get rid of it? Ameliorate or humanize it? What do we mean when we say, Where super-ego was, there ego shall be?

We sometimes answer the question of super-ego time too violently. We try, as Ann Marlowe says she once did in her marvelous book *How to Stop Time*, to *fully* escape temporality. Her drug of choice for time-stopping was heroin—which delivered her from the anxious pressures of time but left her existence a blank. She could not move forward with her art, her writing, her life. She could either stop time with the drug, or be overwhelmed by the anxiety-creating demands of time and the super-ego. There was no middle ground. Says Marlowe at the end of her book:

> The life heroin bestows is not less painful just less profound;
> not less stressful, just less surprising. And while dope does
> stop time, it also stops beauty. After I quit, it gradually came
> to me that the messy stuff I'd been screening out with dope—

the nitty-gritty of having a relationship, constructing friendships, getting along with acquaintances, meeting new people—the stuff that hadn't seemed worth the trouble, the stuff that had to be controlled so I could focus on the important matters, was in fact the only material life presents. While I was nodding off over my computer or exploring the metaphysics of a rock band in some East Village club along with other initiates with pinned eyes, the people who didn't do dope were actually out there, unprotected by opiates, having experiences, often difficult ones, but indisputably real, uncontrollable, sometimes transcendental, and always offering that possibility, which heroin rules out, of something AMAZING happening that will change your life forever.

Time for Marlowe was, we might say, all Chronos and no Kairos. Chronos is the dull, grinding wheel. Kairos might be broadly described as a desirable experience of time that stands in some dialectical relationship to Chronos. The privileged moment, the epiphany, the descent of the muse, the visitation of the spirit, the sudden joy in being, the vision that flashes upon the inner eye with the bliss of solitude: insofar as these temporal, antitemporal experiences exist, they refute the omnipotence of mere Chronos. But in a culture that cannot provide instances of Kairos, broadly understood, Chronos rules forever and time is created in the images provided by the super-ego.

The only ready way to fight super-ego time is to try to kill the sense of time the way Marlowe does—with a drug that blots out anxiety, until it wears off. But Marlowe's obliteration of time with heroin is different from the redemption of time, to which she refers at the end of her book. And the redemption of time and of the super-ego is surely what we seek.

Beauty and the Super-Ego

Is beauty a good defense against the tyranny of the super-ego? Strange as it sounds, it may be. To look into the mirror and be pleased is no small matter. To be judged beautiful, or at least highly attractive, by those around you can be of genuine consequence. The approval of the Other, and the approval of the self for the self, can strengthen the ego. It's irrational, of course. Why should anyone love himself the more for being physically attractive? But we do.

All of what Freud called ego-syntonic experiences boost the strength of the self and make it less susceptible to super-ego criticism. Denounce me all you like, hate me as you will: the mirror disagrees with you. I am absolutely fine, so mind your own business.

But to be homely, ill-favored, or in some way deformed: these are not ego-boosting states. The ego cannot love itself so readily or so well then, and as Freud says, "to the ego, living means the same thing as being loved." The individual may go in search of other forms of approval. He may achieve professionally; he may seek fame; he may make his name in one way or another: these activities can compensate for a depleted love of self, and they may make the subject less susceptible to the anger of the over-I. The larger and more complex the ego is, the better its defenses against the world, against others, and against the pain inflicted by rogue authority.

Jacques Lacan, as we've seen, pictures the child entering what's called the mirror stage. He sees the composed, attractive image in the glass and loves it. But he himself lives with internal discord. His needs and desires make his interior being turbulent. He's a creature of lack, confusion. And there in front of him is a beautiful, composed self that he cannot become identical with, no matter how hard he might try. Probably he'll spend his whole life painfully pursuing the united being he sees before him. And as Lacan sees it, he'll never coincide with his ideal.

But perhaps this is not quite so. Young people often do seem to blossom into a beauty that occasionally allows them to take themselves as their own ideal. They are content to *be*. They do not need to *do* much of anything to be happy with themselves. And it seems their super-egos leave them alone, or at least back off a step.

How much do we enjoy it when the person who can love her mirror more than any being out in the world finally comes crashing down? She sees that she has been wrong, evil, hateful. And now she must repent. This is the story of the Hollywood celebrity who has ignored all the loves that approach her, out of love for herself. Then her looks fade, the drugs exact their price, enemies conspire against her. Or, it's the story of the pro ball player, who had the world in thrall with his knife-sharp passes and his power to baffle tacklers and take the ball in on his own. Then we hear about the drugs, and the assaults

But in time: Look, there they are on the front page of the tabloids, mouth open, eyes dazed. And sorry, sorry, sorry. They're sorry for all the people they hurt and all the damage they did. The super-ego, once knocked from its throne, has come striding back and taken dominion. Off to rehab, to therapy, to religion. But soon they'll be back—the comeback gig, one more chance—tempting fate again, wooing the crowd, and for now holding the old toxic king at bay. We love the rise and we love the fall: what could be better entertainment?

People pursue beauty and strength. They work out, do yoga, take up excruciating diets, lay out for cosmetic surgery, spend half their gross personal product on appearance. (Been in a drugstore lately? In large part, it's a store for appearance enhancers.) Self-beautification is the order of the day: and if others elsewhere risk starvation while we repair the damages wrought by time or increase the advantages bequeathed by genes, then so be it. By so doing we can perhaps defend against the ravening super-ego.

Once in a seminar I heard Harold Bloom ponder Freud's observation that "the ego is a bodily ego." Bloom thought quietly for a while and then came up with something: when you go off to be fitted for clothes, you stand in what's called a three-way mirror. With one look you can see yourself from the sides, the front and the back. The feeling you get when you see that is a sample, quite an intimate one, of how you feel about your ego overall. Bloom concluded his riff with admirable dash: "Though I may be marvelously ill-favored, I would never wish to change my physical form with that of anyone else." I believed it. Give or take.

"Modern exercise," says Mark Greif in "Against Exercise," "makes you acknowledge the machine operating inside yourself." From Greif's vantage, contemporary exercise is a function of the super-ego. We have a routine. We record every moment of exertion carefully, we have goals, and when we don't meet them we become despondent. When we miss a day of exercise, we receive the proper super-ego punishment. In order to defeat the super-ego with beauty—or at the least not being homely, or marvelously ill-favored—we conform to super-ego–like regimens.

The common explanation for our efforts to cultivate strength and beauty is that we wish to stay, or become, attractive to others. We want to find a new mate, summon a slew of admirers, or at least confirm the affection of the mates and admirers we might have. All that is probably true. But I think we also pursue beauty, or at least physical improvement, in the interest of our internal lives. If we can like what we see in the mirror, we can enhance our ego strength and fight off the tormentor just a little more successfully. For how can the super-ego hate what is beautiful?

Yet one must remember, there is nothing so painfully transient as beauty. "Death," says Wallace Stevens, "is the mother of beauty," meaning in part that what gives beauty its allure is the fact that it will soon fade and then, all too quickly, disappear. And the door is again open to the sadistic super-ego. The one who has cultivated looks and little else will have few resources to defend against the new dispensation. Our culture is devoted to the cultivation of good looks, in part to keep the super-ego at bay. Ultimately this is not a winnable game: time and chance happen to us all.

Patriarchy and the Super-Ego

Freud often gets a bad rap for his dealings with women. Did he misunderstand female sexuality? He surely understood what many of his contemporaries did not, which is that female sexuality *exists*. Women have drives; they have desires. The cultural suppression of women's erotic lives caused considerable sorrow in Freud's time. Many of the women Freud treated were ill in part because they had been compelled to deny their wants. And Freud came to understand that. As a therapist and theorist, he may have done more to free women (and men) from sexual oppression than any other single individual. He understood that sexual desire and the quest for a satisfying erotic life are at the core of nearly everyone's being, male and female. He made that understanding public, sometimes at the cost of sharp criticism, and it's helped to make many, many people happier—or at least less miserable—than they would otherwise have been. Freud was willing to tell the world what it didn't want to hear: that women had orgasms and could enjoy sex. The distinctions he drew between clitoral and vaginal orgasms, seeing only the latter as legitimate and mature, now make little sense. But Freud championed female sexuality, and at the time at least, that meant he championed women.

Most members of Freud's inner circle were men, but the circle included women too. One of them, Marie Bonaparte, was probably his closest friend during his last years: he was fond of her personally, and he respected her mind and her psychoanalytical writing. (He also collaborated with her in translating a book she had written about her chow Topsy—Bonaparte and Freud loved dogs.) She helped Freud get out of Vienna after the Nazis annexed Austria: without her intervention, he might have died a horrible death in a concentration camp, as four of his sisters did. When it was time to choose someone to replace him and to continue the work of psychoanalysis, he did not choose one of his male disciples or one of his sons (he did not think them terribly creative), but a woman, his daughter Anna.

Freud's view of women was in many ways constructive, but not entirely so. If there is one idea of his that it probably would have been good to retract, it is surely the idea of penis envy. Little girls see a boy's penis and they want one themselves. They are jealous. They feel that they have been denied by nature—they're not what a human should be: their self-confidence collapses and they never truly recover. Freud believed this strongly. The doctrine of penis envy was still with him late in his career, potently articulated in the manuscript he left unfinished when he died, *An Outline of Psychoanalysis*.

Freud was almost always capable of intellectual development. On the subject of homosexuality, for instance, he changed. Early on, he saw homosexuality as a pathology. Homosexuals were people who had not fully negotiated the Oedipal complex. But his view shifted, and later in his career he came to believe that the greatest problem for homosexuals was not painful psychological limitations, but society's inability to tolerate them humanely. In a letter to the mother of a young homosexual man who hoped that Freud might *cure* her son, Freud wrote, "Homosexuality is surely no advantage but it is nothing to be ashamed of, no vice, no degradation; it cannot be classified as an illness; we consider it to be a variation of the sexual function." It is hard for us now to imagine how unusual this sentiment was in 1934. Here Freud was well ahead of his time and entirely for the good. But on the subject of penis envy, he did not budge.

Freud might have mitigated the penis envy theory by attaching it to the historical and cultural conditions of the time. He could have said that what women desired when they longed for the phallus (if they ever did) was male cultural and economic power. But he didn't. As long as there had been women and men, he claimed, there had been envy of the penis. No cultural change could transform this fundamental condition. Therapy might allow a woman to deal better with its effects, but that was all, and it was not very much.

For someone as intellectual as he was, Freud had shrewd instincts. One is surprised that he did not entertain another possible truth: that neither gender envies the other very much. We all seem to possess a slightly irrational pride in our sex: men delight in being men, women in being women. We seem to nurture a baseline pride in simply being who and what we are. But Freud thought that women wanted to have what men had, be what men were. He sometimes suggested that a woman is by her nature an inadequate being. She longs for the penis; she is envious; she is generally (but not always) nonintellectual; she never develops the same attraction to ideals that men do: the list goes on.

A strong political movement requires potent simplifications. It thrives on identifying villains and exalting heroes. To the women's movement, Freud was a villain. There was little incentive to arrive at a dialectical sense of Freud: such activity, satisfying as it might be intellectually, would not feed the passions necessary to bring about major social change. In this case the change was salutary. The expansion of human possibility that came with feminism remains a cause for celebration. And surely the women's movement is not all that contributed to Freud's eclipse: another cause was the discovery of biological factors in diseases, such as depression and schizophrenia, that he and his followers attributed entirely to psychodynamics.

Still, I believe that two rights have collided to create more than one wrong. Freud got suppressed—that's one wrong. And though the women's movement richly continues, progressive politics overall now proceeds without much psychological sophistication. The astute Juliet Mitchell tried to fuse Freudian thinking and feminism in an engaging book called *Psychoanalysis and Feminism*, and there are still feminists and still progressives who are interested in the dynamics of the psyche as conceived by Freud, but they are a minority. The dominant idiom in American culture now is narrowly political: every other way of talking and thinking is subsidiary. Political concepts have their value, but many of them badly need to be complicated by a psychological perspective.

Freud's theory of the super-ego dramatizes his relationship to patriarchy—and that relationship is more complicated, and more promising, than one might guess. Women, Freud tells us, generally never develop as strong a super-ego as men do, because their passage through the Oedipal complex is less inflected with violence. They are belittled for not possessing a penis rather than bullied into submission by the traumatizing prospect of castration. Which may mean that they are less likely to suffer from raging over-I's in the way that men often can. Their sense of good and bad, right and wrong, may be less draconian and more sane. They may have more freedom to reason and judge outside the *reasonable ravings* of the over-I. They may be a bit freer.

Terry Eagleton observes that it can appear women are being maligned in Freud's theory of the over-I. But, he says, it can hardly be an insult to say that one segment of the population is less disposed to salute the half-mad leader, and (presumably) not so inclined to aim their super-ego strength at others. "The historical evidence would seem to suggest," says Eagleton, "that women are on the whole less likely than men to come under the thrall of transcendental signifiers, to be hypnotized by flag and fatherland to spout of patriotism."

Freud was in many ways the ultimate patriarch. He believed strongly in the value of authority, especially male authority, and he wielded it as a writer and as the builder of the psychoanalytical movement. There is a famous picture of Freud in which he stands in a three-piece suit, cigar in hand, staring with a monarch's poise into the camera. Harold Bloom said that when he tried to imagine Yahweh, Lord God of Hosts and Creator of Heaven and Earth, what came to his mind was that image of Freud, who looks to be judging all that comes before him, and not leniently: Freud, the ultimate patriarch.

But that is not the end of the story. Freud also developed a form of therapy, about which I'll have more to say in the next section, designed to dispel illusions about authority in general and male authority in particular. In psychotherapy, the patient transferred qualities onto the person of the analyst, and recreated him based on past experiences with love objects and objects of influence. A patient might, for instance, believe his therapist hates him when there is no just cause to think so; judges him harshly when no judgment exists; could solve all of his problems if only he wished to do so. Slowly, patiently, Freud taught the patient to understand how much fantasy material he was projecting. In so doing, the patient might see the expectations he brought to all of his significant encounters with authority in life. The therapist helped the patient bring the authority figures in his life down to earth and see them not as gods in a private mythology but as living, suffering, complex human beings. He taught people to approach these figures the way the Buddhist sages suggest that we approach all people. When you encounter someone, your first thought should be: "He is suffering, he seeks happiness."

By humanizing figures of authority through analysis of the transference, Freud helped his patients develop a clearer sense of what was authentic in their experiences with power, and what was merely projected. It made their minds clearer, their lives a little saner. Psychoanalysis, when it is effective, can deconstruct our fictions of authority. Which should change, if only a little, our sense of Freud. The deconstruction of therapeutic authority can feed the deconstruction of patriarchy. How much patriarchal power is projected by the subject? How much is real, and how much a function of fantasy? To be in thrall to patriarchy is in some measure to be in thrall to the super-ego. Freud invites us to shed our illusions about authority and contend with true power.

How real is patriarchy itself? To what degree do men pragmatically sustain illegitimate authority day to day? And to what degree is that authority transferred to men by women and so based upon illusion? Freud invites women to examine their own investment in male power and thus gain perspective and emotional independence from it.

Freud, we might say, was a grand patriarch who sought the dissolution of patriarchy. In doing so, he served women in their struggles with both patriarchy and the super-ego.

The Super-Ego and Race

If I were standing in a bookstore and saw this book on the shelf, I'd surely open it (its themes coincide with my interests rather neatly), and flip to the table of contents. There I'd see this chapter listed, the chapter on the super-ego and race, and probably jump forward to it. I would be driven by the prospect of encountering taboos and maybe the breaking of taboos. What's this author (this White author) up to? Does he say unsayable things about race? Does he talk about race and I.Q. in an insulting way? Does he dare to say the unsayable word? Does he refer to it? Is it in a citation? Is it in a joke? Or does he just up and say it straight out?

And if he does, what shall I, the reader, do? Shall I report him to the chair of his department or maybe the university president? Shall I grab my cell phone and demand to speak to human resources immediately?

I think it no exaggeration to say that the (fictive) super-ego in this (fictive) individual has taken control of his psyche and is calling the shots. Race can do that, here in the third decade of the twenty-first century, loaded as it is with taboos, loaded as the culture is with those who like to enforce them.

Hypocrite lecteur—mon semblable—mon frère: Read on with an open mind, if you can.

Who is the Black man?

In terms of White Mythology, a phrase of Derrida's that has its applications here, the Black man concentrates the appetites. He is a

THE SUPER-EGO AND RACE

roving, relentless id. He seeks pleasure and ease. Work is his aversion, sex his primary vocation. He is a magnet for drugs that, if you're feeling bad will make you feel good, and if you're feeling good will make everything even better. In other words, do just what the super-ego doesn't want you to do. In the White Mythology, Black men are a race of Falstaffs.

In the White imagination, the Black man is all too often an object of both envy and disdain. He's the White imagination's solution—a false solution—to the riddle of the super-ego. The White person can at once envy the Black man for escaping the strictures of the over-I and hold him in civilized contempt. Thus the cultural importance of the Black gangsta rapper, who says, does, and embodies no end of forbidden pleasures. He calls his women bitches and gives them the back of his hand if they act up. He does drugs at will—always ready to light up a blunt. Money? He's got plenty and spends it freely because there's always more. The image of the Black gangsta rapper reaches back to the urban bad man: Bad, Bad Leroy Brown, Staggerlee, and Billy the Lion. Greil Marcus describes him as "an archetype that speaks to fantasies of casual violence and violent sex, lust and hatred, ease and mastery, a fantasy of style and steppin' high." Today, he is the figure who freely busts the taboos the over-I enforces, taboos on drugs and sex, and pleasure without labor, immune to punishment. Plenty of Blacks presumably immerse themselves in the gangsta rap mythology, but the primary audience is White.

Through rap, White kids can acquire a temporary passport to the zone of imagined Black excess. A mixed-race student I know told me that when he and his White friends were driving around listening to rap, they besieged him with a question: When the forbidden word comes around in the rap, can we say it, can we chant it, can we, please? Please? The kids wanted to have the right of Blacks—the right to articulate the forbidden sounds. But they wanted to do it with permission, satisfying both their fantasies and their indwelling agency of authority. What could be better?

The operative emotion is ambivalence. The spectator revels in the rapper's license, loves his louche world and wants (or wants to want) it for his own. But the audience member also takes pleasure in his sense of superiority to the display that both draws and repels him. He hates what he loves and loves what he despises. Both id and super-ego offer their remarkable satisfactions. This ambivalence on race has been part of American life for a very long time.

In his book on blackface minstrelsy, my former colleague Eric Lott pointed to the ambivalence that historically invested the form. Watching Whites in blackface cavort on stage—sing and dance and make vulgar jokes—let the White audience look down on Black life. But, Lott argues, there was also envy, affection, even love for the way of life enacted on stage. The super-ego judged; the id enjoyed. Both sides of the psyche got a hit. Lott writes, "The minstrel show was less the incarnation of an age old racism than an emergent social semantic figure highly responsive to the emotional demands and troubled fantasies of its audience." At the center of that social semantic figure was the White audience's deep ambivalence about what it was seeing on stage: "It was cross-racial desire that coupled a nearly inseparable fascination and a self-protective derision with respect to black people and their cultural practices and made black face minstrelsy less a sign of white power and control than about panic, anxiety, terror and pleasure."

The Black man as the man without a super-ego, the everyday Falstaff, is a prevalent American myth. I hardly need mention that it does not reflect reality. Hypertension, stroke, heart disease, mental illness, early death: all of the afflictions that arise from a too-active super-ego (though they may arise from other causes as well), are prolific among African Americans. They too, of course, face their inner judge.

W. E. B. DuBois speaks of the twoness of African-American life, meaning the need to maintain a double identity, one based in the Black world, the other negotiable in the White. The internalization of White standards, DuBois suggests, causes no end of pain. His famous passage continues to illuminate, more than a century after he wrote it. "It is a peculiar sensation, this double consciousness, this sense of always look-ing at oneself through the eyes of others, of measuring one's soul by the tape of the world that looks on in contempt and pity. One ever feels this two-ness,—an American, a Negro; two souls, two thoughts, two unrec-onciled strivings; two warring ideals in one dark body, whose dogged strength alone keeps it from being torn asunder. The history of the American Negro is the history of this strife,—this longing to attain self-conscious manhood, to merge his double self into a better and truer self."

Private life for the African American takes place behind what Du-Bois calls "the veil," the sphere of being that Whites never penetrate. In front of the veil, the Black person must be something other than what he or she is. And in the splitting there is pain, as there is in being a fantasy object of the White world—the one on whom prohibitions and demands have no effect. In *Black Skin, White Masks*, the Lacanian Frantz Fanon also sees a splitting of the Black self. The Black subject trying to negotiate the White world must affirm the false and oppres-sive authority that wearing the White mask requires.

"Looking at oneself through the eyes of others"—"measuring oneself by the tape of the world that looks on in contempt and pity": this is an exteriorization of the problem of the over-I. Both Fanon and DuBois attest that White consciousness and White judgment can dog Black people through their days. It would be entirely unsurprising if this dynamic were at work in the interior lives of African-American people. It would be anything but unexpected if their mode of oppres-sive super-ego were constituted, at least in part, by the voice of White judgment.

Meanwhile, within this psychological circuit, the White persona acts both as inhibiting, punishing judge and as a spirit that affirms and encourages whatever form of Black misbehavior, real or imagined, it might wish to see. The White force, both psychological and social, makes twin demands of the African-American subject: this subject must be both stiffly righteous and gratifyingly appetitive.

For dwellers in the world of social-justice advocacy, matters seem a bit different. Here the imagined African American functions as an unassailable authority. One must never question the judgment of a person of color. No White person could possibly understand more about the conditions of Black life than a Black man or woman. Even if facts are on the other side, the Black person's view is always correct. All must yield to the superior super-ego authority. Is it necessary to say that being cast as a form of absolute authority is also a form of oppression—and also of extreme condescension? Does one have to add that the subordinate position taken up by the White subject is destructive of his human dignity and powers to think with independence and accuracy?

There are genuine racial problems in America and all through the world. But we would be in a far better state if we did not complicate them with various modes of externalized psychic conflict. If we could stabilize our fulminating super-egos, we might come just a little closer to seeing the world as it is and being able to make it slightly better. As long as the regressive dramas of the psyche condition the public realm, progress of a collective and humane sort is nearly impossible.

PART THREE
Fighting Back

Crack a Joke

One of the more remarkable facts about Freud is that early in his career, he paused to write a lengthy book about jokes—*Jokes and Their Relation to the Unconscious*. It's a thick, meaty book, full of Freud's favorite jokes (not all of them funny) and an analysis of what makes them work. A joke comes from the id, says Freud. It's an eruption of forbidden or at least questionable appetites and desires. Jokes allow the desiring self some freedom to express itself. Jokes can save us from completely bottling up our desires. They function much as dreams do: something forbidden comes out in indirect or suggested form. The dream uses the techniques of dream censorship—condensation and displacement—to encode its messages. Jokes use compression and speed—the potentially offensive matter is there, then it's gone. Jokes also use context. The stage the comedian stands on is a protected space, a secular temenos if you like, from which he can say and occasionally do things that are otherwise forbidden.

Joking is all about the assertion of the infantile self. It's about our desires, often our selfish desires, for food, drink, freedom, sex, the suffering of others, and the right to laze around. Jokes can also express our aggressions. What's funny about a joke is that it gives vent to what we have often felt but been far too tightly wound to express. Society gives special latitude to jokes: the stand-up comedian, as the court jester of our age, acquaints us with truths that we recognize as such but have been unable or unwilling to express. Jokes, like dreams and slips of the tongue, allow what is forbidden to be heard. A joke is an act of decompression: it loosens some of our inhibitions and it makes us a bit freer than we were before the comedian entered the room. With jokes, we can outwit the ever-censorious over-I and even the occasionally prohibitive I. The joke lightens the ego's burden of keeping things under control. A good joke is a small bit of psychotherapy. Where ego and super-ego were, there jokes shall be.

Jokes excite laughter, but of a certain sort. When the humorist admits to some wayward impulse, she must do so with skill. She must do it in a way that allows the laughter of recognition and assent. When we laugh at the joker's exhibition of desire or aggression or what have you, we are saying, Yes, me too; that's just the way I feel and have felt. Or I can imagine feeling so, and I endorse it. We laugh together because together we have bound ourselves up just a little too tight. Society demands that it be so.

Joking is a rebellion (usually a rather gentle one) against the ego and super-ego. The humorist is allowing the id to escape the strictures of the over-I and the ego by ribbing them. Oh how ridiculous you are, with all that you prohibit. It's too much—let's have some fun. And maybe sometimes the over-I concedes the point and gives some ground. Ross Gay, the American poet, has a charming poem called "Ode to My Inner Puritan," in which he acknowledges the Puritan super-ego, teases it a bit, and finally gets it to wander down to the river with him, take off its shoes and socks, dunk its feet in the water, and relax. Maybe we all should try that.

Whether the Rogue King himself is amused by humor is an intriguing question. Maybe he is. Maybe he wants to relax for a while and kick back, too. Though surely we can, with an overly free deployment of comedy, agitate the over-I and also the over-I's of the people around us. Then we've gone too far; the world is not ready for this joke. When Lenny Bruce made heart-attack jokes directly after

President Dwight Eisenhower suffered one, his loyal audience was stymied.

Joking is rebellion from the bottom. It's an assertion by the "lower" part of the human against the "higher." It reminds the over-I that no matter how high-minded it may be, there is another part of life that one denies at one's peril. One Lacanian diagnosis is that such and such a patient desires to have no desires. His super-ego wishes his id to go away and stay away. But the belly and the balls will always be present and will have their say. Without Sancho Panza, Don Quixote goes nowhere and is far less interesting. "Dost thou think that because thou art virtuous," says Sir Toby Belch to the super-ego–ridden Malvolio in *Twelfth Night*, "there will be no more cakes and ale?" There will be cakes! There will be ale! "Aye and ginger will be hot in the mouth."

The now-forbidden Woody Allen is, in Freud's terms, a master of jokes. And they have a particular focus: many are geared toward deflating a cultural ideal. "I don't want to achieve immortality through my work; I want to achieve it by not dying." The ideal getting a gentle tickle here is the ideal of artistic purity. I write only for the future. My goal is to live posthumously. OK, says Woody—but there is something I'd like just a bit more. "The most beautiful words in the English language are not 'I love you,' but 'it's benign.' " Romantic love may be a joy, but staying alive comes first. God? He's not evil, says Woody; the worst thing you can say about him is that he's an underachiever. A soft, but not too soft, dig at religion—a word from below. Woody specializes in this sort of thing—taking the air out of inflated ideals, outfoxing the ego and super-ego. Is this habit, perhaps, rebelling against the spirit of the age, a part of the reason he has been cast into disgrace?

That's joking; humor is something else. Freud describes it in a very short paper written well after the book about jokes. With humor we effectively and voluntarily take the place of the super-ego. Freud's first example is of a condemned criminal who is to be sent to the gallows on a Monday morning. "Well," he says, "that's a fine way to begin the week." Freud sees that the man has the same regard for himself, his life and his death, as his own super-ego and the cultural super-ego as well. He is looking down on himself as from a great height and mocking his own predicament. So what if a worthless person, a criminal, has to die. The world will continue to spin.

The ability to look down on oneself this way, Freud says, is the mark of a superior individual. He understands his own inconsequence in life and sees himself as the world sees him. He looks upon himself and upon the collective life as an adult looks upon the doings of children. Humor, Freud tells us, is a way of saying, "Look, here is the world, which seems so dangerous! It is nothing but a game for children—just worth making a jest about."

Many people can take a humorous attitude toward others. Says Freud, "the subject is behaving towards them as an adult does towards a child when he recognizes and smiles at the triviality of interests and sufferings that seem so great to it. . . . Thus the humorist would acquire his superiority by assuming the role of the grown-up and identifying himself to some extent with his father, and reducing the other people to being children." But the higher art, according to Freud, is the ability to stand in a father's relation to oneself.

Maybe there's more to it than that. Maybe the subject is not just usurping the place of the super-ego but also mocking it. It's as if he is saying, This is how you see me, this is how you see the world. But how inhumane you are, how bitter and small. The condemned man is not mocking himself so much as he is mocking that within him that dislikes him enough to revel in his death. He is making a parody of his super-ego. A fine way to begin the week? This is what a part of me would say. This is what some region of the self would assert. But that region is small and cruel and worth all the mockery I can muster.

How far do jokes and humor take us in the struggle with the super-ego? Some way, I think. They engage in a guerilla war against the tyrant by signaling awareness that his way is not the only way. They're constantly suggesting that the cruel emperor has no clothes, or at least is dressed very badly.

Part of the reason that we so need company, I think, is to find a context for our humor and wit. We want to show others that our war is ongoing, and in their laughter see a rebuttal against stale injunctions and deadening prohibitions. Jokes matter. Humor matters. (Richard Rorty once said that the true purpose of pedagogy was to teach students to laugh at our jokes.) Our jokes and dashes of humor are radio bulletins sent out from an occupied country to whoever might choose to hear. They are signs of resistance, antidotes to quiet desperation. But they will probably not lead you to a new life in a culture of the super-ego.

Laughter creates community, though. When we laugh with a friend in an unfeigned, joyous way, we solidify likeness of mind and of soul. We create a small pocket of resistance to the hegemony of prohibition and restraint. For an instant, we become one of those "ironic points of light" that, as Auden said, "flash out, wherever the Just exchange their messages."

Get Lucky

Freud once remarked that there's an easy way to get the super-ego to back off and to treat the ego (the you that is you) better. This method is simple, available to virtually everyone, and sometimes doesn't cost a nickel. It works for men, works for women, and if you are a kid with a swollen over-I, probably can work for you too.

The simple remedy is this: get lucky. When you get all the breaks, or a lot of them; when you win big at cards, get the promotion you deserved (but only more or less), find out that you've inherited a pile—your ego swells. To use the current idiom, you feel good about yourself. To be a little more precise, you feel like a favored being, like someone dwelling in the light, a mortal blessed by the deities. When you get lucky, you take it as a sign of your own superior qualities, and the ego enlarges. Life loves you and you love life in return. Recall that Freud told us that to the ego, living is the same as being loved. When you get lucky once, or encounter a string of good luck, it seems as though the universe is in love with you. And the universe is stronger than the super-ego—or most super-egos. Says Freud, "The field of ethics, which is so full of problems, presents us with another fact, that is that ill-luck—that is, external frustration—so greatly enhances the power of the conscience in the super-ego. As long as things go well with a man, his conscience is lenient and lets the ego do all sorts of things: but when misfortune befalls him, he searches his soul, acknowledges his sinfulness, heightens the demands of his conscience,

imposes abstinence on himself and punishes himself with penances."
"When things go well," the super-ego must back off.

We are, apparently, rather primitive beings. We cannot believe
that luck is just luck. We cannot believe that our good or bad fortune
is often based simply on chance. We seem to think that we have done
something to deserve it. I suppose that on some level we have. We
were in the right place at the right time when we could have been
home in bed, clenched beneath the covers. We did the deed that
Woody Allen said was necessary though not sufficient for success: we
showed up. You have to put yourself in position for luck if you hope
to get lucky.

If matters go well and our number comes up on the big wheel, we
owe it all to ourselves. Our ego swells, gains in strength, and readily
holds the over-I at bay. Good luck is a hit of steroids for the self. The
ego puts on muscle, gains endurance, and is ready to contend with its
chief adversaries: physical life, other people, and of course the super-
ego. The individual hits the streets with a bounce in her walk, speaks
with authority, demands what she desires, and sometimes gets it.

Why do people go to Vegas? Why gamble? For a million reasons,
of course. They go to cash in. Go to make some money. They go for
the diversion and for the sex, paid for and not. But I think there's another reason: to do well, to get lucky, swells the heart. It's not just that
you fill your pockets with doubloons until they spill on the floor, and
you can buy this or that or the other thing. A winner, particularly in
games of chance, has been blessed by the gods. She's got the kiss of
heaven on her forehead. Her ego enlarges and she feels an outward
confidence. And an inward strength too. See, she can say to her super-
ego, I'm not the hopeless loser you say I am. I'm special, blessed, a
winner through and through. Every time we try to get lucky, we are
trying, among other things, perhaps many other things, to get the
over-I to back down. Luck is always on the side of the big battalions,

Napoleon said, or maybe it was Voltaire. When we get lucky we believe we command extraordinary force and forces.

"Getting lucky" has other connotations too. How much sexual adventuring is an effort to prove one's attractiveness, one's appeal, one's worth? You see, she loved me. I must be something special and good. I'm not what my inner self insists I am. In one of Freud's reflections on erotic life, he says that the lover puts the beloved in the place of the inner agency of authority. What she approves of is gold—and she approves of him: more than approves, she adores him. Using the lover as surrogate super-ego is an effective strategy, Freud says, but it's also limited. Soon the beloved falls out of love with you; she may even turn against you. No criticism is quite so sharp as that which comes from a beloved who at one time praised your every act and word. Now she's taken on remarkable authority as a super-ego substitute, and even her simplest criticisms cut with an uncanny sharpness. Having merged with the super-ego, she has taken on some of its power.

Oh for those halcyon days when all her judgments were appreciative, loving. She created a rapprochement between super-ego and id. Her presence was vitally ego-syntonic. Now matters can go either way. She can instill peace in the psyche or foment strife. Why is love so alluring? For many reasons, not all having to do with super-ego dialectics. But one cause is the hunger for deliverance from internal criticism. We wish to be loved by another because we are in no position, no position at all, to love ourselves. (Something within us refuses.) Adam Phillips cites Jacques Lacan's perplexity at the Christian injunction to love our neighbor as we love ourselves. To begin with, most of us don't love ourselves all that much. Perhaps we often treat others as we treat ourselves—meaning not terribly well.

When people who loved us withdraw their love, or calibrate it, the ego feels the cold blast. And then too, our luck runs out. And since we are primitive enough in our inner selves to believe that good luck is our doing, we are also prone to feel that being unlucky all comes back to us. I'm not worthy of being a winner; I don't have the stuff, we say, even when our failure has little if anything to do with character or skill.

As high as we have mounted in delight, in our dejection we sink as low—maybe lower. Luck runs out and we bottom out. In the erotic sphere, we find we can't "get lucky" anymore. We can't believe we are worth much. When the roulette ball hits the wrong number time and again; when one potential lover after the next hangs up the phone, erases the email, or junks the text, the ego shrinks and we enter a world of meek despair. Says Freud, "If a man is unfortunate it means he is no longer loved [by Fate]; and threatened by such a loss of love, he once more bows to the parental representative in his super-ego—a representative whom, in his days of good fortune, he was ready to neglect."

In short, there may be no more effective way to short-circuit the super-ego than by going out and getting lucky. It's perhaps the best weapon at our disposal—though alas, it's really not at our disposal at all. You can decide you're going to put yourself in luck's way, go to the casino, hit the party, or show up at the bar at closing time, and see what happens. The problem is that getting unlucky—and often we do, especially when we press the case—only makes matters worse. As high as we have mounted in delight, in our dejection do we sink as low—and maybe a lot lower.

Freud knows how important luck can be, but he offers another remedy for the inflamed super-ego. So-called civilized people become much more cautious and dutiful when they are feeling unfortunate. Says Freud, "It is remarkable how differently a primitive man behaves. If he has met with a misfortune, he does not throw the blame on himself but on his fetish, which has obviously not done its duty, and he gives it a thrashing instead of punishing himself." If someone were to invent an effective, up-to-date fetish for the over-I's subjects, it would be no small boon for humanity.

Get Drunk

At the center of the psychoanalytical world view is a defining perception. To Freud, we are not unified beings. We are defined by internal conflict. The psyche is usually in a state of civil war—sometimes loud and violent, sometimes quietly grating. Its various agencies never see matters in quite the same way. They have divergent goals. One part of us seeks the satisfaction of need and desire; one part seeks perfection, or at least social obedience; one part seeks to mediate between those two, and also to navigate the always complex, occasionally quite dangerous outside world. Thus, to Freud, *character is conflict.*

Inner conflict hurts. The collision of various desires creates anxiety, confusion, and a sense of unease. We would like to be all of a piece. But to Freud, character is agonistic—and it seems he might be correct. We all would like to end our inner conflict, but how?

One of the most effective ways of dealing with inner dissension is meditation. Carl Jung says that with meditation we calm the unconscious aspects of the mind, which would mean both the id and superego. By focusing on our breath, letting go of intruding thoughts, and repeating a mantra, eyes closed and attention evenly suspended, we effectively hypnotize the unconscious and bring it to a dreamlike state. Jung implies that this is not an entirely productive activity, since it causes us to lose contact with the deeper mind, which is to Jung, as it is to the Romantic poets, potentially creative. But if your goal is to calm the psyche, meditation is a completely viable way.

But most of us haven't time for meditation or can't be bothered to learn how. Some find the feeling of calm it creates to be a little sterile. And it doesn't last forever. (In my experience, twenty minutes of meditation gives me about twenty of tranquility, thirty renders thirty and so on down the line. At this rate, I'd need eight hours a day to approach anything like Buddhist composure.) But there are other ways to calm the psyche's tensions. Almost certainly, the most common is alcohol. For some reason—and no one really knows the chemical dynamics of alcohol consumption and metabolism—the effects of drinking often include inner harmony. The agencies seem to flow together. Alcohol affects everyone a little differently, but I think that people who drink—especially one drink or two—seek calm, acceptance of what's going on around them, and self-acceptance, too. Alcohol often delivers.

Alcohol seems especially effective in quieting the super-ego. After a glass or two of wine, we're not quite so hard on ourselves. We love ourselves a little more, or at least don't dislike ourselves so much. The psyche melts together, the super-ego quits its badgering, and our desires get more chance to make themselves known and maybe even get some satisfaction. In short, we loosen up. Character is suddenly not defined by conflict.

It lasts a while, of course, this relative unanimity of the psyche, but not forever. The poet George Herbert tells us to stay away from the third glass, but it's not so easy. We want to stay where we are: high. We want to be *above* the inner dissent that is an integral part of day-to-day being, and above the workings of the world. We want to look upon life the way a good-humored adult looks upon the doings of children. But the third glass often doesn't do it: we go flat and become resentful, irritated. We can mount a bit, but then down we come. And yet we have tasted genuine deliverance from the super-ego, and from conflict. We have attained what few humans can for any extended period, unity of being. But it doesn't last. What George Carlin said of cocaine is true of booze and most other pleasure-inducing drugs. "Cocaine, great stuff. Makes a new man of you. Only one problem, new man wants a hit." Alcohol cannot adjust reality; it can only adjust our relations to reality.

Alcohol is a many-faced drug. The god most closely associated with intoxication is Dionysus, who seems to have the power to assume nearly any shape he likes. Just so, there are numberless words for alcohol—booze, hooch, tipple, toddy, juice—and even more names for being drunk: smashed, loaded, stiff, bombed, pickled, plastered, ripped, and on and on. But if I were to select a single synonym for alcohol it would be one of the most common and surely one of the more sedate. "Spirits" seems to me to come closer than any other term to the core of the experience.

Isn't that what alcohol bequeathes? Spirits. It elevates our vitality, plumps our vigor, and gives us more juice and jam. Alcohol is a muse of fire. It burns away what is mucky and slothful in us. It takes what is airy within and turns it to crackling potential power. Spirits: it's not for nothing that Homer's warriors dose themselves with wine. It intensifies the passions, restores courage. It reignites the desire for ascendancy after it's been subdued by the rough resistance of the world. Sometimes alcohol raises the spirits too high; then we get mayhem: broken bottles, busted hands, a brilliant new car wrapped around a pole, a face face-down in the street.

But most of the time, alcohol gives us more gumption, more confidence. It pushes us across the room to talk to him, talk to her. It lets us pop off in public—at a sedate dinner party, maybe—surprising our friends (and ourselves) with the artful exuberance of our opinions. (Has there ever been anyone—with the possible exception of Plato—who knows all of what he thinks on a given subject until he hears, under the influence of a warming glass or two, what he actually has to say?) Dionysus is also known as Luscious, the Luscious one and the Liberator, and alcohol can be exactly that, a breaker of the bars on the self-designed jails that too many of us inhabit too much of the time. Alcohol may have inspired the splendid Fiona Apple tune with lyrics that go, "Kick me under the table all you want / I won't shut up; I won't shut up."

With alcohol, we can become just what the super-ego does not wish us to be: lively, confident, open. Spirited!

But after spirited unity comes the morning after. The hangover is an incompletely understood experience. Most of us think it is the aftermath of an encounter with a toxin. Alcohol is poison. The word "toxic" is enclosed inside the word "intoxicated" like a tarantula in a gift box.

So to many, the morning after is about dealing with the aftereffects of the poisons. But there may be more to it. The pain we feel in the morning might also arise from the reassertion of the super-ego as it reclaims its dominant place in the psyche. It does so, sometimes, through exerting its power to humiliate us. All of the excesses and misdeeds, however mild, of the previous night come before the judge's bench for trial and censure. The ego is castigated for being so permissive, wayward, undisciplined. The super-ego grows in strength. Do we need a remedy for that? Another drink might do it.

As David R. Lenson puts it in his outrageously good book *On Drugs*, "The aftermath of the high is therefore more than a physiological reaction, more than headache and nausea. It is also the vengeful rebuilding of all those barriers the drug was able momentarily to dissolve." Alcohol dissolves the barriers between desire and moderation, between aspiration and judgment, and sometimes between I and another. Come morning, those barriers need to be rebuilt, and what we feel is the loud and ugly clanking of the reconstruction job.

It's interesting to contemplate how much of what we call culture might consist in self-intoxicating ways to evade the super-ego, at least briefly. We go to movies, play video games, watch this or that series on TV, even occasionally read a book. Those activities have the capacity *to fill the mind.* That is, we allow various productions to take over and replace the content of the psyche, and when they can do that, we rate them very highly. We call them good shows, good books, good plays, because they have delivered us from ourselves. They are what are broadly called escapist. But whether the most sophisticated text is any less escapist than a cheap film—that is an interesting question. It matters, I suppose, how the individual makes use of them. Still, the alacrity with which we surrender our psyches to other forces should make us reflect on how dismaying the basic content of self may actually be.

Are there other ways to solve the problem of the super-ego, other ways to achieve inner unity? There are, I think, though they may demand more from us than we have to give.

Take a Pill

What is serotonin? Technically speaking, it is a chemical produced in the body that bathes the brain in pleasurable sensations. It produces the feeling of well-being. Serotonin discharge comes as a reward. When we do something good, we get a squirt or two. When we finish the task, make the last payment, win the game, win all the games, the chemical, we are told, bathes the brain and we feel renewed. It seems we have to earn serotonin. And we require it to keep us from unhappiness, maybe despair.

But sometimes we cannot generate enough of this needful substance and the result is anxiety, depression, sorrow. So we take a pill, a selective serotonin reuptake inhibitor (SSRI), and perhaps feel a bit better. The serotonin we produce doesn't disappear so rapidly from the brain, leaving us bereft. The drug, at least in its design, is ego-building. It fortifies the self against its antagonists. It helps the ego to stand up against the slings and arrows of everyday life, against illness and disease, and presumably too against the ravages of the super-ego. The ego must be artificially strengthened to do its job in the world.

Does it work? It seems to, better at least than a placebo. The self on antidepressants seems better able to function in the world, able at least to get out of bed and meet the demands of the day, or some of them. Serotonin stays around, isn't absorbed back into the body, and that gives the subject a certain boost, not the radical jolt of cocaine but a continuing baseline sense of assurance. The individual can function in the world, and that's far from a small matter. A major discovery, antidepressants; they've probably saved many lives that would have otherwise been lost to total disfunction, and maybe to suicide.

They don't work for everyone, of course, and they don't work forever. All over the developed world, men and women sit in offices, often rather elegant offices, and meet with patients for fifteen minutes each. How are you feeling? Better than last week? Worse? How is your sleep? What kind of appetite do you have? Sex? Questions answered, the doctor perhaps tweaks the prescription, or maybe decides on a new one altogether. A drug that has done yeoman duty for years suddenly fails to deliver. A new drug comes on the market. Let's try that. An extra-stressful week? Take some anti-anxiety pills on top of the SSRI—the benzodiazepines kick in quickly. Though there are addiction problems with them, rather brutal ones.

The ego is a garrison under siege, and reinforcements need to be dispatched to this or that quadrant of the fort. Problems abound, and the solution often lies with a better drug regimen. Everyone wants a new drug, and what you want, you usually get. Patients are up on the latest research; they follow the trends in the major news outlets and even in medical journals. They talk to friends about how they are managing to lift their ever-dragging spirits. Then they repair to the doctor's office and petition for the latest. It's a collaboration between healer and sufferer. Maybe there is a drug out there that could not only raise the spirits but unlock the limitless potential that is there—it must be—in the college-educated middle class.

The self-sustaining drugs no doubt fill many functions, but at least one use, perhaps their chief use, is to provide reinforcements in the war with the super-ego. When the super-ego demands too much, when it lashes the ego without mercy, when it practices all kinds of cruelty, the self has little to fall back on. Exercise? I can't get out of bed! Talk to friends? They can't bear me—all I talk about is my depression. Deepen your marriage? I lost that long ago. It's just me and my drugs and my ravening over-I, which my medicine man and I hold at bay as best we can.

And the side-effects are not pleasant. It is far from uncommon for the subject to lose his sex drive, or hers. Years go by without arousal, intercourse, orgasm—pleasure leaves. In its place there is a life that tastes a little too much like cardboard. So there is impotence. There is a quiet sorrow. And there is the slightly weary, flattened-out feeling that comes with life on the drug. Yet society at large does not understand that the super-ego probably plays a prominent part in almost all cases of anxiety and depression. It hits the ego so hard that the ego, the self, needs reinforcements. It calls in mercenaries. But mercenaries have a way of getting out of hand, stomping off the job, or slipping away into the night, and the self has to live with the results.

Is there a better way to deal with the crisis of the super-ego than medicating it? Is there an alternative to the quiet somnambulism of the moderately drugged post-modern psyche?

Get Religion

Religion, Freud famously observed, is the longing for the father. It's not only that, of course.

Freud also says that religion is an illusion, a belief we sustain based upon our wishes. It's not an error or a mistake or a misapprehension. An illusion is based not upon the way that the world is, but on the way we wish it were.

Yet an illusion can turn out to be true. A middle-class girl with no particularly distinguished qualities may believe that one day she will marry a prince. She may hold this belief with the greatest fervor, never letting go of it under any circumstances. It is an illusion. But the fact is that she may actually marry a prince. The odds are long, but there is a tiny chance that it will come through.

So it is with the belief in God. We have no scientific evidence that God exists; there is no empirical reason to believe in him. But still, there he may be. To Freud, the God illusion, like all illusions, needs to be dissolved so that we can see life as it is and act accordingly. The responsibility to better the world rests upon no one but ourselves. Stop looking skyward for help and begin looking to yourself.

God is an illusion, but to many a very important one. We need to believe there is life after death. We need to believe there is a meaning to our suffering and that in time, suffering will be redeemed. We need to believe that some larger force cares about who we are and what we do, moment to moment, day to day.

We also, Freud suggests but never quite says, need the presence of God to stabilize our inner lives. God may vie with our super-egos to impart laws and judgments to the psyche. His presence, imagined or not, may actually lighten the burden the super-ego places on us. The biblical God can be harsh, but there are limits to his harshness. He is a jealous and punishing presence, but one may reach some form of peace with him and his dictates. He issues his commandments, and his churches and temples disseminate and interpret them. So one can perhaps live righteously.

In short, we can know in broad outline what God wants. Within the Judeo-Christian world, we have the commandments sent by God to Moses. How should we behave? Worship the Lord. Have no other gods before him. Keep holy on the Lord's day. Do not covet thy neighbor's wife, or his goods. Don't commit adultery. There is a measure of clarity here about how to live and what to do. Granted, books upon books have been written to teach us the true nature of the teachings. But in the Holy Book, one can find in compressed form a rendering of the will of God. The doctrine is fairly stable.

One of the problems with the super-ego is that it is variable, irrational, and ever-changing. It is also unconscious. One does not always know how to please it. Perhaps it cannot be pleased at all. The believer can understand Yahweh, at least in some measure, and know with a moderate certainty what he requires. (Though a reading of the book of Job may rattle our certainty on that score.) If one puts Yahweh in the place of the super-ego—if one actually *can* put Yahweh in the place of the super-ego—then some confidence and certainty may result. But of course, you can only internalize God in this way if you truly believe.

With religion invariably comes ritual. In the Catholic Church, for example, these rituals often take the form of sacraments: baptism, communion, confirmation, marriage, holy orders, extreme unction.

Each sacrament marks a passage from one stage to another. The child who receives communion is now in charge of her own spiritual destiny. Her sins are true sins and may send her to the infernal zone. To be married in the Church means obeying the Church's laws about fidelity and commitment. Every sacrament guides the communicant from one state of being to another, in which she will be subject to new demands and achieve new satisfactions. The sacrament introduces the individual to the law of the Church. It inducts her into a set of individual commitments. But the attendant ritual is aesthetically pleasing and collective. There are the communion dress, the communion suit, the communion breakfast, the gifts, the photographs, and the blessings. Ritual beautifies and humanizes the law's demands and demonstrates the law's collective application: this is not only asked of you but of others too, who will help you stay your course when need be. Ritual makes the law mild and even sweet—at least to the true believer.

Many people now have no real ritual in their lives. My students celebrate their birthdays as though they were monarchs of some small but prosperous duchy. They love Halloween and New Year's Eve. But most of them are far too secular to enjoy faith-based ritual. They celebrate Christmas as a time for good meals and commodity transfer. Easter does not exist except as a basket of chocolate chicks and rabbits for the young ones. If you don't have a round of rituals attached to some form of benevolent authority—the sort that, as Hannah Arendt describes in her essay, you accept without question—you gain in freedom, but you lose an element of stability from your life. You are set radically adrift, and accordingly you are vulnerable to the cultural super-ego, which seems to manifest itself wherever there is an authority vacuum.

It's possible that Nietzsche had it wrong. The idea of God has lost authority for many and become genuinely untenable. Perhaps those people are truly liberated. But perhaps they are simply left with the problem of the super-ego, which is no smooth and easy fate. For the rest of humanity, those whom Nietzsche doesn't account for, belief in God and the teachings of the Bible, the Koran, or what have you, may be a completely satisfying possibility. It can be enriching in itself. And it may solve, or begin to solve, the problem of the rogue over-I.

Freud's major book on religion, *Future of an Illusion*, is probably his most optimistic piece of writing. He says it is possible for humanity to pass beyond belief in God and take responsibility for its own welfare. Where God was, there our god, science, shall be. We won't worship science, but we'll use it to do the one thing that matters most in culture—cut down on needless suffering.

But maybe humanity needs both God and science. Our adherence to the laws of God—harsh but not too harsh—may generalize and stabilize what would otherwise be a bitter super-ego. Such belief would let us know where we are in the world. For God, as the West understands him, is not a ghostly father figure but an emblem of fate and necessity, of the law and of the miracle that is the world and the miracle that is the universe that contains it.

For those disposed to belief, the question is clear: Why not fill the God-shaped hole with, well, God?

Get a Shrink 1

Is it possible to cultivate the super-ego? Make it less wildly demanding, more civilized, more sane?

The difficulties are clear. The super-ego is unconscious, at least in large part, and it is not easy to communicate with the unconscious. Nor is the unconscious easy to influence. The agency wants to keep itself to itself—that is part of its power. It never comes into the light fully and willingly, is rarely seen directly, face-to-face. It's a god that hides behind its clouds and makes that hiding a principle of its authority.

But Freud suggests that the therapist can influence the over-I. He must do this thoughtfully, humanely, but do it he must. The question is how.

I've talked about the way various individuals and groups have dealt with the pressures of the super-ego. One of the most common responses is to put something or someone else in its place. Sometimes this can be productive, other times not.

The man or woman in the crowd puts the leader in the place of the super-ego. At times this can bring about concerted, humane effort. What Churchill and Roosevelt accomplished as wartime leaders was invaluable. But all too often, the leader does not coax forward the best in his followers. As Freud tells us, the members of the crowd are often hypnotized by the self-absorbed, charismatic man on the platform. They become less aware, less critical—unwilling and maybe unable to think for themselves. They undergo mass regression and become children under the rule of a paternal stand-in.

There is always the chance that the individual will come to regret what he's done under the sway of the political over-I. How many citizens of Germany and Russia, loyal to Hitler, loyal to Stalin, came to look back in horror at the deeds they performed under the leader's influence?

Freud also observes that the lover can put the beloved in the place of the super-ego. Suddenly the over-I becomes less judgmental, kinder, maybe even complimentary. But if (when?) love fades, the subject is left hypervulnerable to the beloved's criticisms. If she turns fully against him, she manifests herself as an embodiment of the over-I at its most punitive. Falling in love as a cure for super-ego malaise is risky. One takes one's chances that the new over-I may become as destructive as the old—and be beautiful and alluring to boot.

What about therapy? Is it possible that in therapy the patient may put the analyst in the place of the super-ego? There are reasons he might be tempted to do so. The therapist is, without doubt, a figure of authority. You come to him; he is the one who's paid; he possesses the license and the advanced degrees. At their best, therapists are understanding, decent, humane, and above all tolerant. They believe, along with Freud, that there is much more to understand about human beings, and less to judge, than society and the super-ego believe. The therapist is not without an ethic. But it is likely to be more tolerant and decent than the one the patient, aching from the ministrations of the over-I, brings to the office.

If you are suffering from the ravages of the super-ego, most therapists are likely to tell you, usually indirectly, maybe on occasion overtly, to lighten up on yourself. But to the sufferer that may be beside the point. Others have told him this too. If he could take advice from friends, even well-meaning, experienced friends, he would not be sitting mournfully in the therapist's office.

But the therapist often simply embodies a more sophisticated and tolerant morality that, over time, communicates itself to the patient. She is accepting, never shocked, never moralistic. Her persona takes on authority in the patient's psyche. Over time—and therapy can last quite a long time—the therapist, and all she represents by way of the tradition of psychotherapy, might actually become a constitutive part of the patient. She may, in other words, be put in the place of the super-ego, or at least her presence may revise the super-ego.

Conducted in this manner, therapy is not unlike teaching. The therapist is in the position of an instructor who aims to offer an alternative version of life and how to live it. The therapist would gradually install herself, and all she represents, in the mind and heart of the individual the way that an especially influential teacher of English or philosophy might do. The pupil senses in a great or good teacher the terms and values that might change her life for the better and embraces them. In this case, the patient becomes a proponent of the ethos of psychoanalysis and lives with more balance and satisfaction than she otherwise would have done.

And yet there are objections. Can a rational human ethos, even if administered by someone in authority, displace or even revise a force as stubborn and elusive as the over-I? Maybe it will work for a day or so after a session. Maybe it will work for the duration of the treatment. But how well can such mild-mannered intervention last over time? Granted, as Freud says, the voice of reason is a small one, but it will not rest until it gains a hearing. If the therapist's voice does manage to be heard, and even affirmed, there are still potent forces, internal and external, to shout it down. Intellectual influence may not be enough to revise the super-ego.

Then there is this: Freud's ethos is an ethos of autonomy. He would be very unhappy if his work were reduced to a doctrine, communicated like any other, that chiefly engaged the intellectual faculties. The imposition of terms and values from outside the individual is anathema to the spirit of analysis—even if the terms and values are analytical and come from the analyst. No, one must seek salvation on one's own. One may be guided by the teacher but must not be ruled by his teachings. Anti–super-ego pedagogy is too confining and robs the patient of his freedom. Plus, it may not work.

Are there alternatives?

Get a Shrink 2

If the id manifests itself, so too might the over-I. To Freud's way of thinking, the id badly wants to communicate, but the force of repression holds it down. Despite this censorship, the unconscious does what it can to make itself present. In his beautiful elegy, "In Memory of Sigmund Freud," Auden describes the way Freud enjoins us to be "enthusiastic over the night" and its "delectable creatures," who look at us dumbly, asking us to take them into the daylight world. "They are exiles who long for the future / That lies in our power." They are manifest in dreams, in slips of the tongue and pen, in jokes, in sudden expostulations, and in behavior that initially seems rather inexplicable. The objective of analysis in the early phases was to listen for the murmurings of the unconscious id.

In free association—the continuous stream of talk that holds nothing back—Freud found a way to contact the unconscious. The patient entered into a state of mind between sleep and waking, and allowed his thoughts to flow freely. There, the therapist encountered the substance of what had been repressed. Sensitively, gradually, he revealed it to the patient or allowed the patient to see it for himself, and if all went well, some gain in awareness arose. For Freud, of course, a gain in awareness is always a gain in psychological health.

Freud in the early phase also analyzed dreams—making his way, with the patient's help, from the manifest content to the latent. If all dreams are disguised fulfillments of repressed wishes, then with careful analysis one might find one's way to the fundamental dream impulse. Such an approach frequently bore fruit. But later in his career, as he was coming to terms with his "discovery" of the super-ego, Freud began conducting analysis in a different way.

He became a student of what he called "the transference." The more he practiced therapy, the more he came to see that patients transferred material from encounters with individuals earlier in life onto the person of the physician. Without the patient's knowing it, the doctor became a stand-in for mother, father, brothers and sisters, and lovers. The analysand treated the therapist not as he was in and of himself: of that she generally knew little. Instead she transferred other identities onto him—and surely among the most common was the identity of authority figure. For many patients, the doctor came to stand in for the super-ego.

When the patient was defiant, or unproductively passive, afraid of punishment or abasing herself to curry favor, the physician was in a position to see how she was prone to comport herself in the face of authority in her life and how she might comport herself in the face of her own super-ego. When a patient insisted on constructing the therapist, who until that point had been mild and rather detached, as a figure of punitively cruel authority, then it was clear that the session had entered the realm of the transference. This was a fine turn of events: now the transference could be analyzed. Through understanding how she constituted the therapist, the patient could begin to learn the nature of her own super-ego and her relation with it. By understanding that her over-I was especially crude and regressive, the patient might begin to put its demands in context and treat them with intelligence and maybe a measure of irony.

"Ah yes," she might say, when she is feeling profoundly self-critical, "I know that voice; it's the voice of the rogue over-I. I recognize it; I'm not without respect for it, but I've seen how susceptible I am to it. I'm not going to let it run my life, at least right now." When the patient goes out into the world and finds herself projecting nefarious powers and intents onto figures of authority, she may be in a position to recognize what she's doing and free herself, if only by so much. When she quivers with guilt at the recollection of some past infraction—sin of omission, sin of commission—she might be able to say, "Sure, I have this irrational side. I see it. I take note of it and take it seriously. But I know that despite wearing the cloak of rationality, it is irrational in the extreme. It goes in for punishment. It's sadistic. It raves reasonably. And so with a respectful nod, I dismiss it." The super-ego is a price we pay for having a highly developed civilization, and it's got to be respected. But bow to it? No.

Could transference therapy diminish the powers of the over-I? I believe it might. One of Freud's most promising ideas is that awareness of the repressed diminishes its determining power. By reading this book and taking the concept of the over-I seriously, you may have already diminished its powers, if only slightly. To cite Adam Phillips again: Where super-ego was, there ego shall be.

Carl Jung was no Freudian, but he did give voice to at least one strong Freudian perception: the psyche, he said, must learn to make deals. That's something far different from what Jung seemed to treasure most, connecting with the archetypes. Deal-making is far more pragmatic, worldly, even market-oriented. Yet what Jung said may have some bearing on the situation of the over-I. Richard Rorty cherished the ideal of conversation: the exchange among individuals that he saw as central to sustaining civilized life. In *Philosophy and the Mirror of Nature,* he describes conversation as the crucial element in the education of the self and others. He uses the German word for education and personal growth, *Bildung.* This process, Rorty feels, needs to continue throughout an individual's life. "To see keeping a conversation going as a sufficient aim of philosophy, to see wisdom as the ability to sustain a conversation, is to see human beings as generators of new descriptions rather than beings one hopes to be able to describe accurately."

Perhaps it is possible to develop an art of *internal* conversation, along the lines that Rorty describes for *external* exchange. Maybe the various elements of the psyche—call them by their Freudian names or by monikers of your own—could enter into dialogue with each other. What does each side of the self want? What will it give up to the others in exchange? No lasting peace will ever come this way—if Freud is right, the psyche is always full of tension. The conversation, as Rorty says, will never be resolved, and the quest for resolution is probably futile. We will never be well once and for all. Character is conflict. But maybe, in time, one can become adroit at this exercise. Maybe the psyche could learn how to make deals.

PART FOUR

Beyond the Super-Ego

Embrace the Ideals

Human history gives us a template for values that might genuinely displace the rogue super-ego. But these values are so difficult and demanding that associating them with normative terms like *ego-ideal* and *super-ego* and *sublimation* is an impoverished way of thinking. There is nothing easy or pedestrian about the great ideals.

Since human history began, men and women have stood in awe of three pursuits: the pursuit of wisdom, the pursuit of bravery, and the pursuit of compassion. We celebrate these qualities and try to cultivate them within ourselves. When we see them embodied to the full measure in some individual, we stand back in awe. The compassion of Jesus, the courage of Hector, the wisdom of Plato and Socrates: these are large achievements, and many if not most of us look to them with vast admiration.

Those who follow the path of the ideals enjoy the chance to attain difficult joys that most of us never taste. The pursuit is dangerous. Socrates and Jesus and Hector all died violent deaths.

Hector may be a legendary figure (or not), but he stands in for all of the actual warriors who have given their lives so that their nation or people might survive. Homer's Hector is decent and humane, yet he is also a formidable fighter, willing to lose his life to protect his family and the city of Troy. And so he does.

Socrates too dies violently, at the hands of the Athenian state. He is the thinker who will question anything and everything. In time, his constant enquiry angers those around him, and they put him to death. But Plato comes along after him to pursue the truth. And in his magnificent philosophical works, he lays out a vision of the best of all possible lives. Philosophy thereafter is what Alfred North White-head said it was, a footnote to Plato

In the West, Jesus stands as the ultimate figure of compassion. In his teachings and in his life, he embodies humane love for all. Love the Lord thy God with your whole heart, soul, and mind. Love your neighbor as yourself. The Hebrew Bible teaches us the first of these commandments; the Gospels teach the second. The Jesus of the Gospels is kind, thoughtful, inventive, and brave. The Romans saw that he was there to topple everything they believed in and valued. They had ample reason to do away with him. Yet his teachings came to inspire their world, and for the better.

Now let us be more precise: what exactly is meant by ideals?

I can answer this question better with examples than with abstractions. The examples will come from literature, philosophy, and religion, the areas I know best. These are moments—three of them—that fascinate and move me, and that have never failed to move my students. Some have felt admiration and awe when they've encountered these moments; others were unhappy. But no one was indifferent.

One of these moments comes in Homer's *Iliad*. It's a scene that involves the Trojan hero Hector, his wife Andromache, and their baby boy Astyanax. Hector comes striding in from battle, his bronze armor filthy and covered in gore. He's wearing his helmet with its great horsehair plume. Andromache runs up to greet him, but his son, who's being held in a nurse's arms, explodes in terror. Who is this giant, this monster? Who is the terrifying man? Hector hears his boy's cries and immediately understands the cause. He lifts the great bronze helmet from his head. Immediately the boy stops crying and jumps into his father's arms.

Hector is a magnificent warrior: the Trojans have no better or stronger one. But as we see, he is also a father and a loving husband. He and Andromache talk together as the scene unfolds, and it is by far the most intimate and loving conversation in the poem. Hector, we find out, believes he will die in the war with the Greeks (which he will). But he knows still that it is his duty to defend his city. He'll do it with a high heart and as much intelligence as he can muster. Hector knows something else as well: he is not a natural warrior. I have *learned* to stand in the front ranks and not to falter when the enemy comes forward, he tells Andromache. He had to learn how to be a fighter; it did not come naturally to him.

His depiction in the poem bears this out. We sense that as great a warrior as he is, he would have been better still as the city's prime minister, and in time, after the passing of his father Priam, as its king. He can be calm and restrained. Helen, the supposed cause of the war, says he and Priam are the only men in Troy who treat her with courtesy. Yet Hector sees that he has been born into a time of war, so a warrior is what he becomes. He risks his life and eventually loses it in the struggle to defend others who are weaker than he. That the struggle is a losing one—the Greeks of course take Troy—does not make Hector's efforts any less noble. It even makes them more so.

Hector is a citizen soldier. His first calling, it seems, is to a life of peace. But when war comes, he steps forward, though he has to acquire the warrior craft—unlike his great antagonist Achilles, who is clearly a born fighter. Hector is the archetype of all of those men and women who, though they would rather live peacefully, step up when they see their country threatened. They are ready to sacrifice their lives to defend themselves and defend others.

The troops who went off from America to fight World War II were almost all citizen soldiers. When asked, they seldom said they were out to rid the world of fascism or conquer evil. They were inclined to say that they wanted to do their jobs and come home. But beneath their modesty there was a gallantry not unlike Hector's. They were ready to die for their country and their friends. Thousands of years of history and literature tell us that this willingness to defend a noble cause is one of the highest callings a human being can answer. It is an ideal. Granted, the ideal becomes difficult to pursue when it is not clear to what degree the purported enemy actually threatens one's nation, or that the conflict at hand is just. But it pays to consider the ideal of bravery, to respect it, and to be open to engaging it.

People who commit themselves to the life of military honor can—and sometimes do—live with a fullness and intensity that those who serve only themselves cannot imagine. The ideal of honor is not only alive in the military. Firefighters and policemen and -women are called upon to be ready to give their lives for others, and sometimes they do. At the end of a life in business, a man or woman may have made millions of dollars and have invested it well. A firefighter may have saved three or four people's lives by pulling them from burning buildings. Which of them rests more comfortably at the close of life?

Are policemen and soldiers and all who commit to the heroic ideal susceptible to corruption? Of course. Some policemen have taken bribes and worse. Soldiers fail to do their duty. In some cases they do worse than fail: they fight dishonorably; they commit atrocities; they let their buddies down. Ideals are always susceptible to corruption and fraud. People claim they have done heroic deeds when they have not. They pretend to be great soldiers when they are at best mediocre ones. But as common as fraud and corruption are, the genuine ideal continues to glow brightly. Human beings want their lives to matter, and one of the ways they achieve this is by committing themselves to bravery. They commit themselves, they struggle, and some reach the ideal. They may not reach it every living moment: but surely there are men and women who embody the heroic ideal and often do so with considerable modesty. It can be hard to believe, but ask the ghosts of the fascists in Germany and Japan and Italy who not that long ago tried to enslave the world—ask them if it's not so.

The marvelous moment in the *Iliad* when Hector commits himself to go on defending Troy, despite his fears and despite the fact that he was not entirely made for war, concentrates one ideal, the ideal of courage. But the military ideal isn't the only one. There are peaceful and humane ideals as well. One of those is glowingly manifest during a moment in the trial of Socrates, as Plato, his great pupil, relates it to us.

Socrates has been accused of corrupting the young. It's said that he has denied the existence of the gods and has been teaching the youth of Athens how to make the weaker argument appear to be the stronger. He's on trial in the Athenian law court, and if he's found guilty he'll be executed.

Socrates is innocent of the charges against him. He doesn't dishonor the gods—in fact he has very little to say about them. And he's not in the business of teaching people how to make slick arguments: that's the game of his archenemies the sophists, who teach in exchange for money, something Socrates has never done. But he has been annoying, to the point of outraging many of his fellow Athenians. Years before the trial, someone had asked the Delphic Oracle a question: Who is the wisest man in Athens? The oracle must have been in a particularly obliging mood that day, since it answered the question directly rather than with its customary riddle. The answer was Socrates. No one in Athens was wiser than Socrates.

Socrates, probably not without irony, said that the oracle's pronouncement shocked him. For he knew nothing at all. His ignorance didn't result from lack of effort. He was a lover of wisdom, he said, and was constantly on the lookout to come to a better understanding of life and answer its crucial questions. But so far, despite all the effort, he felt that he had gotten just about nowhere. Why had the oracle singled him out for his wisdom?

Socrates had to know. He went around questioning the citizens of Athens one by one. He asked them what they thought the good life was; what true knowledge might be; how they would define piety and justice. His fellow citizens thought they knew the answers to these questions. But when Socrates pushed them and posed objections, their beliefs began to look silly. Their thoughts were self-contradictory; their arguments full of holes. You can imagine how popular this made Socrates. Even worse, a group of young men, including Plato, followed Socrates around and listened to his interrogations. They found them humorous. They laughed, probably sometimes guardedly, sometimes not, at what the purportedly wise Athenians actually amounted to under Socrates' questioning. The questioning and probing and bothering that he did from day to day was surely the basis of the resentment that gathered in Athens and provoked his trial. The sniggering of Plato and his buddies could not have helped much either.

At his trial Socrates said he thought of Athens as a thoroughbred horse, strong and beautiful. The horse had magnificent potential and had already done remarkable deeds. But it had a propensity toward laziness and self-satisfaction. Socrates saw himself as a tiny buzzing creature, a gadfly, inconsequential in himself but necessary to keep the beautiful horse from dozing into fat complacency. It was Socrates' vocation to deploy his stinger around Athens: the gods, he believed, wanted it that way.

At his trial, Socrates says that asking questions and helping people to love wisdom and virtue (if they could figure out what those ideals really amounted to) is his vocation in life. He was born to do this. And then he says something outrageous: he can no more leave off asking his questions, buzzing and stinging, than Thetis's son could leave off his vocation, which was bequeathed to him by the gods. Thetis's son is the great Achilles, the archenemy of Hector and to the Greeks the most formidable warrior who has ever lived. Achilles is the "soldier's pole," to use a phrase of Shakespeare's: he sets the standard for Western warriors for all time. Alexander the Great lived to emulate Achilles; Achilles was never far from Julius Caesar's mind.

Socrates like Achilles? How outrageous! Socrates was homely and poor. He had no noble lineage; his mother was nothing like Thetis, a sea goddess. Socrates' mother was Phaenarete, a midwife. His father was a stonecutter. (Achilles' father was Peleus, a king, formidable with his spear.) Socrates was married to Xanthippe, who was forever scolding him and once supposedly became so exasperated with his ostensibly indolent ways that she threw a plate of urine at him. But Socrates says it directly: he is like Achilles in that he has a duty to himself and the gods. And, he suggests, his way of life is no less important than the way of the hero. The quest for wisdom matters as much to the world as the quest to be a hero.

Then Socrates takes a step toward proving it—and this is the moment that I want to emphasize. You might tell me, he says to the court, that if I'd stop my questioning and stinging and wondering aloud, you'll let me go home and live my life in peace. You might imagine that I'd relish the chance to go on living under such terms. But I wouldn't. As soon as you let me loose, I'd be back doing what I do: searching for wisdom. That's my destiny, just as fighting the enemy was Achilles' destiny. So, he continues, if you want me to stop, you'll have to kill me.

Which the citizens of Athens vote to do. They decide that Socrates must die for the crime of thinking for himself and trying to understand who he is, what men and women are, and how they should live in the world. He discovered no answers to these questions. But his great pupil Plato, who liked to follow him around and watch him work on the Athenian bigwigs, did reach some conclusions. Plato kept asking himself the kinds of questions his great teacher had asked, and he finally became satisfied that he could answer them. In doing so, I'm sure he had Socrates in the back of his mind. He wasn't going to let what the Athenians did to Socrates put an end to philosophy. He would carry the game through.

Socrates matters a great deal in and of himself. But perhaps he matters most because he makes Plato possible. Socrates comes on the scene to rid Athens, and through Athens perhaps the world, of over-reaching error. He is the ultimate figure of doubt. But the philosophical ideal entails more than exposing error. It is also about the pursuit of truth. Socrates sets the stage for the pursuit of truth; Plato enacts the ultimate drama of the quest.

How should we live? What sort of inner life is the best? How shall we govern ourselves? What sort of state is the most just? What is the correct relation between women and men? How shall we raise our children? What part does art play in life? What shall we do with and about music and poetry?

In his major dialogues, and particularly in *The Republic,* Plato seeks to answer all of these questions and more. Socrates found that his fellow citizens lived amid incommensurate and misleading ideas, feelings, and opinions. He saw their minds composed of cobwebs, and he blew the cobwebs away. But what to do with a mind that has been fully cleansed?

To Plato the answer is obvious: begin building. Socrates' effort is deconstructive. Plato steps forward into the blank that Socrates has made and begins a grand reconstruction. Doubt is not enough for Plato. He seeks more than irony, more than skepticism, more than worldly detachment. He seeks truth—and not just a truth for the present day or for one class or race or gender, but a truth for all.

Those who follow in the steps of Socrates—or think they do—and spawn only doubt, do not work fully in the best philosophical tradition. The stage of doubt is critical, but men and women cannot live by doubt alone. They need truth, or aspirations to truth—and this truth is the goal of the philosophical ideal: there is no ideal higher.

Everyone after Socrates and Plato who seeks knowledge is their heir and owes them gratitude. Whenever a young person pursues truth with the aim of helping not only herself but other men and women, Socrates and Plato are somewhere out there in the ether, rooting her on. Every humanist who tries to tell the truth about the world she sees before her and how it might be a better place is an heir of Plato and Socrates. But every scientist who works to end disease or develop our powers to feed ourselves or drink decent water is too. Those who pursue learning so as to improve the world are heroes: they are as noble as the son of Thetis. Socrates indicated as much, and he was right.

Are the pursuers of knowledge often self-seekers and frauds? Of course. And if we are honest, we see that sometimes their motives are split between the desire to help humanity and the hunger for fame— "that last infirmity of noble mind," as Milton calls it. But I believe that no thinker has ever done work of major merit without being motivated on some level, perhaps too deep for ready perception, by love of humanity. Of course it is tempting to put on the cloak of wisdom and pretend to be an all-knowing figure, even when one is far from it. The temptation is augmented by people's yearning for figures of authority, leaders and wise men who will absolve them of the burden of thinking for themselves. Humans readily fall in love with what one psychoanalyst called "the subject who is supposed to know." But that does not mean that the world doesn't contain legitimate, unselfish strivers after knowledge.

The life of the hero and the life of the thinker have, for us in the West, their prototypes in ancient Greece. But the third of the great ideals makes itself manifest four hundred years after the death of

Socrates, and not in Rome, then the center of the world, but in Jerusalem. The ideal of compassion was not unknown before the time of Jesus Christ of Nazareth. The Buddha lived five hundred years before Jesus, and the Hindu wisdom that he drew from went back much further. Both the Buddha and the Hindu sages taught versions of the gospel of compassion, but in the West we owe the ideal of loving kindness to the thought and teachings of Jesus.

Jesus was a great teacher, not entirely unlike Socrates or Plato. What he taught was a way of life guided, as he says, by two simple edicts. Love the Lord God with your whole heart and soul and mind: that is the first. That is a radical compression of wisdom of the Hebrew Bible, a book that had been abroad in the world for a very long time when Jesus was born. But the next edict is something new: Love your neighbor as yourself.

Overcome your selfishness, Jesus said. Overcome your tribalism. He tells the story of the man beaten and robbed and left for dead in a ditch. Others pass by and do not help him. But there comes along the road a Samaritan, a man who is not of the wounded man's tribe. They are strangers. The Samaritan owes the man in the ditch nothing. But he takes him up, binds his wounds, and puts him on the back of his own animal. The Samaritan helps the wounded man to an inn, where he installs him in a comfortable room. He leaves money for his care and his lodging and promises to return to see to his welfare.

Jesus tells the story to a lawyer who has asked him a simple question: What do you mean, teacher, when you say, Love your neighbor as yourself? After Jesus tells the story he turns to the lawyer and asks him: Which man was the true neighbor to the poor man in the ditch?

The young man or woman who devotes their life to compassion is trying to be a neighbor to the world. She feeds the hungry and takes care of the sick and comforts the lonely and the lost. He tends to those who have diseases; he ministers to those who have been overwhelmed by mental disorders. He calls every woman a sister and every man a brother.

His compassion is a great gift to the world, but it is also a salvation for himself. The compassionate individual does not live in the world in the same way that most people do. She is beyond caring about rank and competition and hierarchy. Everyone is her equal; everyone is potentially her friend. When she walks down the street and looks at a passing stranger, she does not say subliminally, "There is another." She says, "There is me." Most of us live in struggle: we compete and we fight the war of each against all. The compassionate man or woman can be truly at home in the human world.

People commonly say that Jesus was a miracle worker, but are they sure they understand what a miracle is? The Gospels tell us how Jesus managed to turn a few loaves of bread and a couple of fish into food to feed an enormous crowd. How did he do it? Was it magic, a hocus-pocus trick? Maybe it was. But it's also possible that what Jesus did was much simpler and also more complex than conventional magic. Maybe what Jesus and his disciples did, when they saw that great crowd getting hungrier and hungrier, was to share the little food they had with them. What was in the disciples' pockets and packs? A few loaves of bread, a fish or two. And that was all. But maybe when the crowd saw that Jesus and his friends were willing to share everything, they reached into their own pockets. Maybe the crowd became inspired by Jesus's compassion and possessed by it. Maybe they went from being a collection of individual beings into one large and generous being. What had been a crowd became a community. When they looked at people in the group who had up to now been strangers, they said to themselves, "There is me." They said it and they shared their food.

Isn't that a miracle? Is it not a miracle to help people move from self-centered being to compassionate life? Surely it would be a miracle to turn a small supply of food into a great one through magic. But would it not be a comparable miracle, or even a greater one, to help women and men be better than they were only a moment ago?

People who commit themselves to compassion do not produce such miracles every day—they may never produce them at all. But they do help themselves and others shuck off the burdens of self and feel a larger sense of being. Of the three great ideals, the ideal of compassion is the most available. The warrior needs physical prowess; the thinker needs a good mind (though more than that, he needs to be honest); a compassionate person needs only an open heart, and all of us, one might assume, can open our hearts.

Nietzsche all but said that compassionate people were losers. He said that they couldn't compete among the strong, noble people, the warriors, so they set up a new scale of values. They declared that it was better to be mild and vulnerable than to be powerful, better even to be sick than to be hale and vigorous. They used this new scale of values to raise their own status and denigrate the truly noble ones, the warriors. Believe Nietzsche if you like. But before you do, consider immersing yourself in the day-to-day lives of hospice workers and nurses and advocates for the poor. Ask the people who hurt the most in our society what they would do without the few who, out of goodness of heart, have chosen to become their friends.

The embrace of the ideals is arduous at best, deadly at worst. But it provides purpose, unity of self, and a being that experiences itself as existing outside of time. You know what you are supposed to do in the world—the super-ego doesn't have to tell you. Every part of your spirit is directed to your goal: character is no longer always in conflict. You are beyond time because you live not in the present, but in the eternal now that is inhabited by those you want to emulate. The idealist knows what he lives for. He understands how to live and what to do.

These values—courage, compassion, and wisdom—are universal. Though societies may understand them in slightly different ways, they are valued everywhere. Every village and every city has its wise women and wise men. You go to them when you are in trouble and do not know what to do. You go to them to understand yourself better. Or you go to them for a good time—because like Socrates, many of them like to laugh. Brave men and women? Ask around, their neighbors will direct you to them. "Down there, last house on the lane. He's quiet and won't readily tell you what he did. But many are alive because of him who would otherwise be gone. He's melancholy enough. He doesn't sleep well and his wounds, within and without, hurt him sometimes. But he's what you're looking for if you care about that sort of thing." Compassionate people? Common enough in this world, I think. They know that caring for others isn't work but a form of joy. They have nothing, or very little. But when they pass people on the street, they do not say, "There goes another." They say, without thinking much about it, "There goes myself. For that too I am."

The best place for the ideals to thrive is, as Walt Whitman knew better than anyone, in a democracy. Here we can find it easier to be compassionate, for we know each other, as Whitman taught us, to be brothers and sisters. Here we are willing to fight bravely, because what we fight for has great value to us. We fight for democracy, the best chance the world has ever seen for human flourishing. Here we seek wisdom with ardor, because as Whitman told us many times, democracy is an unfolding process. We must develop. Must progress. And honest thinkers and poets like Whitman and Emily Dickinson and Ralph Waldo Emerson are crucial for keeping the great experiment unfolding.

In an astonishing passage in the Preface to *Leaves of Grass*, Whitman creates an image of the kind of large and generous world where the ideals can thrive. "This is what you shall do," the democratic bard says.

Love the earth and sun and the animals, despise riches, give alms to everyone that asks, stand up for the stupid and crazy, devote your income and labor to others, hate tyrants, argue not concerning God, have patience and indulgence toward the people, take off your hat to nothing known or unknown or to any man or number of men, go freely with powerful uneducated persons and with the young and with the mothers of families, read these leaves in the open air every season of every year of your life, re-examine all you have been told at school or church or in any book, dismiss what insults your own soul, and your very flesh shall be a great poem and have the richest fluency not only in its words but in the silent line of its lips and face and between the lashes of your eyes and in every motion and joint of your body.

In a world of free and loving democratic people, the ideals are most worth pursuing, because their pursuit enlarges not only the individual but the community in which he or she lives.

What relation does commitment to the ideals have to the super-ego? I can put it quite directly. Commitment to the ideals can displace the super-ego. One overcomes the super-ego not by civilizing it, not by turning it into an ego-ideal, not by entering into a dialogue with it. One displaces the super-ego by going above it. One installs a standard of behavior that makes the demands of the over-I look childish and small. One becomes more rather than less exacting. One revises the over-I by showing that there is a zone above it that renders it inconsequential. One does not change the super-ego. One transcends it.

You do so in part by being ready to live and if need be die for what you believe. The super-ego fears death and fears life, and wishes you to stay a child. The idealist has no time for small-scale commitments. He seeks a perfection so difficult that it displaces the small-scale demands of the middle-class agencies of order. For that is all that the super-ego is: a manifestation of the values and necessities of bourgeois civilization. Step aside from that civilization, and you will leave its impediments behind.

One goes back in time to the ideals, to go forward to the present and overcome the socially insinuated self. You undergo a new beginning. Where the Freudian structure of self was, there a new, more archaic, and braver structure of self may come to life. One transcends being in the present in order to connect oneself with standards and values that are, or may be, eternal. One overcomes not only the existing self but all of the templates for self that press on every side. The over-I, as Freud admits, is partly a cultural construction. Those who choose the ideals can pass beyond culture into something better.

They are no longer middle-class psyches, or Freudian egos. They have moved beyond the trials of the inner self, its petty tyrannies and small-time civil wars. They are more than the bridge to another form of being that Nietzsche praised in *Zarathustra*. They are that new kind of being, new for being old in the oppressive context of the new.

They have done and do what few human beings can. They have transcended their history and their culture. They have transcended themselves.

Where super-ego was, there human ideals may be.

There, in a thriving democracy, they may be.

Bibliographic Essay

Freud? Freud in 2023?

Why bring up the old ghost? Why revive old factions? And why, in particular, apply Freud to culture and politics? He may, marginally may, still have something to tell us about individual life and the struggles of the individual psyche, but Freud on the larger world, the social world?

I am, for what it's worth, half a Freudian and maybe a bit less. There are weaknesses, to be sure: we all know them, and I've mentioned them in the book. Freud on women is a particularly mixed bag. But mostly Freud fails where we might expect he would. He spent his therapeutic time with people who were suffering badly. They couldn't leave the house, couldn't profess their love, couldn't address a figure of authority, didn't know what they wanted out of life. Freud over time became an anatomist of sorrow, and to me a very good one. He saw how the spirit shuts itself off from knowledge of itself, and he opened pathways for people to know themselves better. This had been a task of the most valuable Western thinkers since Plato.

But Freud—given the company he kept, given his cast of mind— never developed a vision of human happiness, success, joy. Of flourishing he knew little. He had his own success to ponder. It was hard-won and to him incomplete. As a template, it was not enough, though. There are many more ways to thrive in the world than are dreamt of in Freud's philosophy. Freud had no aptitude for perceiving or understanding the ideal. He couldn't generously imagine a life of compassion, of courage, or of unselfish commitment to art. He honored the scholarly ideal, but only as he and a very few precursors embodied it. Schopenhauer and Nietzsche were authentic thinkers, he understood, but he spent all too much energy mildly discrediting them or hiding his debts. He sometimes seemed to think that the West had produced only one real thinker and his image resided in the nearest looking glass.

But as an anatomist of our self-created sorrows, I think that he has no peer. We are our own worst enemies. Most of us do not know ourselves. And the few who do have little power to use what they know. If you want a harsh look at your failures, there is no better academy to attend than Freud's.

Our failures tend to be emotionally based, Freud says. We do not understand our passions and our inhibitions half well enough. And we are creatures of feeling far more than creatures of thought. Whole societies too can become awash in feeling. Sometimes this is all to the good: the emotions that fired free people to throw off fascism during the Second World War are deeply moving. But all too often when emotions take over a culture, the results are not happy. I think that we find ourselves in a period where passion—especially the passion for judgment and condemnation—is at an unendurably high point. Recall Freud's great lesson, as it is compressed by Peter Gay: he taught us that there is far more to understand, and less to judge, than we had imagined before. One might add that there is also a great deal to understand and then forgive. This book is an effort to encourage understanding and forgiveness—compassion and humor.

Anyone referring to the English text of Freud's writing must begin with expansive thanks to James Strachey and his collaborators, who translated and edited Freud's complete works. The volumes are always clear, often elegant, and beautifully indexed and ordered. All praise to the makers of *The Standard Edition of the Complete Psychological Works of Sigmund Freud* (24 volumes, Hogarth Press, 1953–1974).

Peter Gay didn't merely compress some of Freud's best wisdom into an aphorism. He also wrote an excellent biography of Freud, *Freud: A Life for Our Time* (Norton, 1988). The amount that Gay learned, synthesized, and presented in first-rate prose is staggering. Freud's first great biographer, Ernest Jones, is still well worth reading: the book is admiring and generous—and so it should be (*The Life and Work of Sigmund Freud*, Basic Books, 1963). Thinkers like Freud come along very, very rarely: they deserve the benefit of the doubt in at least one major biography.

Freud is also the beneficiary of one of the best books ever written about a thinker's overall views and legacy. Philip Rieff's *Freud, the Mind of the Moralist* (University of Chicago Press, 1979) is a wonderful, generous attempt to synthesize Freud's reflections, finding a more or less comprehensive set of values and commitments through the forty years of Freud's major phase. The only book I know that compares to it is Northrop Frye's study of William Blake, *Fearful Symmetry* (Princeton University Press, 1969).

Harold Bloom often said that somewhere in his attic there lay a yellowed manuscript for a book on Freud, transference, taboo, and authority. I'm heartily sorry that Bloom never published that book; I have no doubt that it would have been superb. I did, though, have the chance to take Bloom's Freud seminar in New Haven, and so learned a good deal about Freud from an oral tradition akin to the one from which I learned about Buddhism. Bloom's approach to Freud in the seminar was often oddly deconstructive: he sought (and found) any number of places where Freud's thinking was at odds with itself. But Bloom being Bloom, a most human presence—as much Falstaff as Hamlet—true insights about Freud's persona and presence came forth regularly. That's embodied in an incident I've mentioned. Said Bloom, "When I imagine Yahweh, it is very difficult. The first image that comes to mind, and I cannot get it out of my head, is of the middle-aged Siggy [Bloom's Freud was often "Siggy"] in his three-piece suit staring at us like the judge of all judges." There was plenty in that remark, about Bloom, about Siggy, and maybe about Yahweh too, but you had to work to draw it out.

Bloom directed my Freud-based dissertation, in his rather relaxed Bloomian way, and helped make sure it passed the jury of the Yale English Department. While I was writing, he referred me to the work of Diana Hume George, whose book *Blake & Freud* (Cornell University Press, 1980) showed me that it was possible to talk about Freud from a literary vantage. It was in graduate school too that my interest in Hannah Arendt, an important figure for this book, developed. I read almost all her work, and *Between Past and Future* (Penguin, 2006) more than once. I also savored Elisabeth Young-Bruehl's book about her, *Hannah Arendt: For Love of the World* (Yale University Press, 2004). A perfect title: Arendt's love for the world and hopes for human happiness come through constantly, though her overall thought, provocative as it is, may never quite resolve itself into a coherent view.

At the University of Virginia, I had the luck to teach three graduate seminars with Richard Rorty, one of them on Freud. Rorty did to Freud what he did to so many thinkers he found agreeable—turned him into an adjunct of Richard Rorty and American pragmatism (see *Contingency, Irony, and Solidarity,* Cambridge University Press, 1989). I fought back a bit, but also took real intellectual pleasure in the endeavor. We had money to bring in guest speakers and I recall particularly impressive sessions with David Bromwich and Shoshana Felman, whom we took out for fried alligator after the seminar was through.

It was just after graduate school that I began following the work of Adam Phillips, from *On Kissing, Tickling, and Being Bored* (Harvard University Press, 1994) all the way to his most recent work, *On Getting Better* (Picador, 2022). His subtlety, wide reading, and writerly grace are well known and celebrated. But what I value most in his work is his simple hope that by reading and writing and pondering life from the psychoanalytical angle, we all might become a little happier and of a little more use to others than we would otherwise be.

Slavoj Žižek? When he's on, he's on: his idea about the super-ego and obscene enjoyment seems to me genuinely illuminating. I first found it in *How to Read Lacan* (Norton, 2007). Camille Paglia's work, especially the magnificent *Sexual Personae* (Yale University Press, 1990), is alive with Freudian intelligence and wit. I never miss anything written by Laura Kipnis (most recently, *Love in the Time of Contagion,* Pantheon, 2022), a fine essayist inspired in strong measure by Freud and ever ready to say so.

Emerson, a tutelary spirit to all my writing, says that it takes a library to make a single book, and surely that's true of this one. No doubt I've left significant works out. And there are also those books that I've moved away from over time. Marcuse's *Eros and Civilization: A Philosophical Inquiry into Freud* (Beacon, 1974) once seemed to me one of the ultimate books on Freud; now it seems, alas, rather naive in endorsing regression to the pre-Oedipal and the "polymorphous perverse." Negative influences matter too, and Marcuse eventually became one for me.

There are times for dark analysis of the surrounding political and cultural situation, and sadly I think this is one of them. But it is never entirely apt to forget hope in the possibility of salutary change. I look in that direction at the close of this book, reflecting on the great and enduring ideals: courage, compassion, and wisdom. I try to do these ideals some justice in *Self and Soul: A Defense of Ideals* (Harvard University Press, 2015). It's that book that has been the most prominent influence on everything I have written since.

Acknowledgments

Many, many thanks to Bill Frucht, my editor at Yale University Press, who provided excellent editorial advice and fine hands-on editing.

Thank you to Jennifer Banks, also at Yale, who first engaged with this manuscript.

And thanks to Harry Haskell, for precise and knowledgeable co-pyediting.

A portion of the chapter titled "Super-Ego Drugs: Adderal and Amphetamines" appeared in *The Hedgehog Review*, Summer 2014. I am grateful for permission to reprint.

Deep gratitude to my family, and to my colleagues, students, and friends at the University of Virginia.